FEARLESS WR

RESEARCH PAPER
W O R K B O O K

PRACTICE PAGES FOR MIDDLE-SCHOOL WRITING

Written by Penny Dowdy
Copyright © 2007 by Spark Publishing

Flash Kids is a trademark of SparkNotes LLC

Spark Publishing
A Division of Barnes & Noble
120 Fifth Avenue
New York, NY 10011
www.sparknotes.com

ISBN-13: 978-1-4114-9749-8
ISBN-10: 1-4114-9749-X

For more information, please visit *www.flashkidsbooks.com*
Please submit changes or report errors to *www.flashkidsbooks.com/errors*

Printed and bound in China

1 3 5 7 9 10 8 6 4 2

NOW THAT YOU'RE IN MIDDLE SCHOOL, ARE YOU WORRIED about the difficult writing projects your teachers are assigning? Does the thought of sitting down to write an essay or paper fill you with dread? Don't be fearful—BE FEARLESS! This Fearless Writing workbook will help guide you through the ins and outs of preparing for, writing, and revising your very own research paper. Are you excited? You should be!

Each activity in this workbook is designed to give you extra practice with all of the elements necessary to write a research paper. Check out the *Fearless Writing: Research Paper Guide*, which details all you need to know to make writing a research paper simple, fun, and easy.

Remember, the more you write, the better writer you will become, so practice, practice, practice! By writing in your free time, you will become more skilled, and those school assignments won't seem so bad after all. Here are some ideas to help you practice writing on your own:

Keep a journal in which you record your thoughts daily.
Write letters to friends and family members.
Write your very own autobiography—the story of your life.

You hold between your hands the key to your new life as a fearless writer. Your days of dreading those writing assignments are over.

LET'S BEGIN!

TABLE OF CONTENTS

RESEARCH WORD SEARCH

Each of the words in the box below are related to writing a research paper. Find each word in the puzzle and circle it.

ARGUMENT	EVALUATE	ORGANIZE	THINKING
BOOKS	EXPLORE	PLAN	TOPIC
COMPARE	INSIGHT	READ	VOICE
CONCLUSION	INTRODUCTION	RESEARCH	WEBSITES
CONTRAST	LEARNING	SUCCEED	WRITING
ENDURANCE	LIBRARY	SUMMARIZE	

X	G	L	K	I	V	K	O	T	W	K	I	L	I	Y	A	A	A	P	C	B
O	K	C	I	E	Y	N	G	J	Q	W	H	A	R	M	J	B	G	N	C	H
D	T	K	Y	C	C	Z	I	N	R	U	S	A	D	U	R	K	I	S	T	Q
G	X	W	A	O	D	O	F	E	G	T	R	J	N	W	E	B	B	H	P	C
M	S	L	Q	V	B	S	M	X	O	B	M	Q	W	L	G	Y	I	K	I	P
J	H	S	F	U	I	U	V	P	I	B	I	S	N	L	V	N	Q	C	L	F
N	F	A	Z	Z	V	C	I	L	A	N	P	C	J	R	K	C	Y	A	C	X
N	N	O	D	J	V	C	O	O	T	R	S	W	R	I	T	I	N	G	U	Q
Y	K	G	Y	I	K	E	O	R	H	X	E	I	N	M	K	V	J	B	A	I
C	W	G	F	C	M	E	O	E	S	B	P	G	G	M	S	Z	G	K	P	R
D	E	K	R	I	O	D	Z	S	S	U	N	Y	H	H	P	P	A	Y	C	T
E	Y	I	W	E	U	N	U	I	Q	I	S	Y	R	D	T	I	I	G	Y	C
W	G	V	L	C	S	M	T	M	N	B	X	D	W	S	L	F	X	V	M	Z
B	G	D	T	N	M	E	W	R	E	A	D	J	D	O	T	Q	P	J	Z	J
N	S	I	X	A	S	A	A	W	R	G	U	M	E	N	T	I	R	H	K
E	O	C	R	R	S	E	V	R	X	S	O	R	K	I	M	Z	F	E	L	V
N	O	I	S	U	L	C	N	O	C	S	T	H	O	Q	X	V	Z	U	A	W
E	Z	V	K	D	S	B	V	H	I	H	D	V	Z	Y	G	J	W	W	S	I
E	U	O	O	N	Y	I	N	F	P	C	R	O	V	T	J	K	A	N	N	U
F	K	C	O	E	T	A	U	L	A	V	E	C	C	N	N	O	Q	D	D	S
T	C	B	B	Z	A	W	I	V	W	Q	J	U	T	T	U	N	X	M	H	B

ASSIGNMENT SUMMARY

When you receive an assignment from your teacher, completing an assignment summary will help you get organized. Complete the summary below to show that you understand your assignment.

Teacher: _____

Topic: _____

Length: _____

Deadline: _____

Typed or Handwritten? _____

Format Instructions: _____

Endnotes or Footnotes? _____

Bibliography? _____

Other Instructions: _____

_____

_____

_____

_____

_____

_____

_____

RESEARCH PAPER PLANNER

Another helpful way to stay organized is to create a schedule of all the steps you'll take in researching and writing your paper. Use the table below to schedule your time before beginning an assignment.

Research Report Writing Tasks	Days Needed	Completed
Create Timetable		
Choose General Topic		
Read to Narrow Topic		
Do Research and Take Notes		
Write Outline		
Write First Draft		
Write Footnotes/Endnotes		
Write Bibliography		
Revise		
Proofread		
Write Final Draft		
Hand in Final Paper		

PERSONAL INTEREST INVENTORY

Sometimes you'll be given the opportunity to choose your own topic on which to write your paper. In this case, it will be helpful to create a personal interest inventory. In the boxes below, write a list of things that interest you to help find a possible topic.

Activities	Events	Goals
_____	_____	_____
_____	_____	_____
_____	_____	_____
_____	_____	_____
_____	_____	_____

Objects	People	Places
_____	_____	_____
_____	_____	_____
_____	_____	_____
_____	_____	_____

Problems	School Concerns	Values
_____	_____	_____
_____	_____	_____
_____	_____	_____
_____	_____	_____

BRAINSTORM

Brainstorming is a method of writing down rough thoughts, ideas, and questions about the topic or subject you already have in mind. Give yourself five minutes and use the space below to brainstorm about a possible topic.

Topic: _____			

FREEWRITING

Freewriting is a lot like brainstorming, except your ideas are written down as a paragraph instead of as a list. Use the lines below to freewrite about a possible topic for your research paper.

Topic: _____

_____

_____

_____

_____

_____

_____

_____

_____

_____

_____

_____

_____

_____

_____

_____

_____

_____

_____

AUTHORITY LIST

Use the table below to create an authority list about topics with which you are familiar. Begin by writing a broad topic in the left box, then get more specific as you fill in the boxes to the right.

Broad Topic	General Topic	Specific Examples

CLUSTERING

Clustering is a way of working out and displaying your ideas in the form of a map, with ideas connecting to similar ideas. Create a cluster in the space below to show what you know about a possible research topic.

Topic: _____

MEET THE REFERENCE LIBRARIAN

Introduce yourself to the research librarian at your local library. Gather the information below to use as a resource when you have questions or need directions in your research.

Name: _____

Address of Library: _____

_____

Contact Phone Number: _____

Hours Available: _____

Services Offered: _____

_____

_____

_____

_____

_____

_____

_____

REFERENCE BOOKS AS SOURCES OF TOPICS

Visit the reference section of your library. Write down the reference books from which you would be interested in reading. Include notes about ideas you have on how you could use each book for research.

Book	Author	Notes

PERIODICALS SEARCH

Look through the periodicals at your library for topic ideas. Use this chart to write the names of publications, issue dates, names of articles, and any notes that will help you choose your topic later.

Publication	Issue Date	Article Title	Notes

KEYWORD SEARCH

When searching for information to help you choose a topic, write down keywords that pertain to the subjects you're researching. Then use these keywords as further searches to find more detailed information about your topic.

Topic: _____

Keywords:

1. _____

2. _____

3. _____

4. _____

5. _____

6. _____

7. _____

8. _____

9. _____

10. _____

11. _____

12. _____

13. _____

14. _____

15. _____

TOO-BROAD TOPICS

The topics below are too broad to serve as successful research topics. Rewrite the topics as narrower, usable topics.

Too Broad	Just Right
Example: Coastal wetlands	Ecology of the coastal wetlands
1. Censorship	
2. Affirmative action	
3. Body image	
4. Global warming	
5. Eating disorders	
6. American history	
7. Basketball	
8. Mammals	
9. Medicine	
10. Rock and roll	

TOO-NARROW TOPICS

The topics below are too narrow to serve as successful research topics. Rewrite the topics as broader, usable topics.

Too Narrow	Just Right
Example: The life cycle of the swallowtail butterfly in the Texas Plains	The life of the swallowtail butterfly
1. The right of convicted criminals to carry weapons for self-defense	
2. The role of the commanders' wives in the American Revolution	
3. Comparing proteins from meat and vegetable sources in the American diet	
4. The cost of filling landfills compared to burning trash in Orange County, CA	
5. The success of experimental drugs on lung cancer treatment in 2001	
6. Carly Simon's battle with stage fright	

FIND YOUR JUST-RIGHT TOPIC—QUESTIONING

Use these question starters to write more detailed questions regarding the topic about which you are interested in writing. Then find the answers to your questions.

Questions	Answers
Who . . . ?	
What . . . ?	
Where . . . ?	
When . . . ?	
Why . . . ?	
How . . . ?	

FIND YOUR JUST-RIGHT TOPIC—TOPIC CROSS

Use the space below to develop a topic cross about the topic in which you are interested. Hint: Your ideas are written vertically down the page with the most interesting ideas in the center. Focus on these more interesting ideas by writing more details on each.

Ideas

Details   **Details**

PURPOSE

Understanding the purpose of your paper will help guide you as you write. Write a brief definition for each purpose to show that you understand the types of research papers you may be required to write.

1. Descriptive: _____

_____

_____

_____

2. Persuasive: _____

_____

_____

_____

3. Cause-and-Effect: _____

_____

_____

_____

4. Problem-and-Solution: _____

_____

_____

_____

5. Compare-and-Contrast: _____

_____

_____

_____

TYPES OF RESEARCH ASSIGNMENTS

Think about the purposes listed below. Then give three examples of topics for each.

1. Descriptive

   _____

   _____

   _____

2. Persuasive

   _____

   _____

   _____

3. Cause-and-Effect

   _____

   _____

   _____

4. Problem-and-Solution

   _____

   _____

   _____

5. Compare-and-Contrast

   _____

   _____

   _____

DESCRIPTIVE TOPICS

A descriptive paper should give a very clear explanation or description on the paper's topic without providing your specific views on the subject. Give a topic for a descriptive research paper for each of the given subjects.

1. Famous Americans

   _____

   _____

   _____

2. Animals

   _____

   _____

   _____

3. A type of artwork

   _____

   _____

   _____

4. A sport

   _____

   _____

   _____

5. A style of music

   _____

   _____

   _____

CONCEPT MAP

Create a concept map in the space below to plan a descriptive research paper. You can use a topic from the previous page. Hint: First write your topic in the center of the page. Place supporting information in the circles that branch out from the topic.

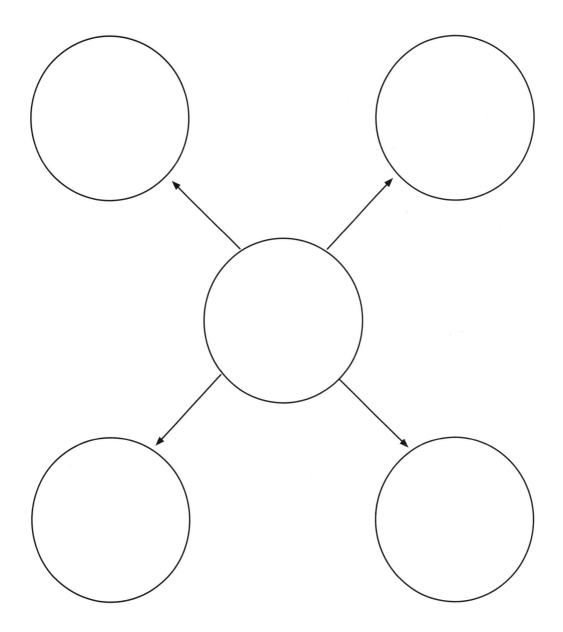

FLOW CHART

Flow charts are helpful for planning a paper that should be presented in time order, as these charts show the order of events. Use the flow chart below to plan a descriptive research paper. You can use a topic from the previous page.

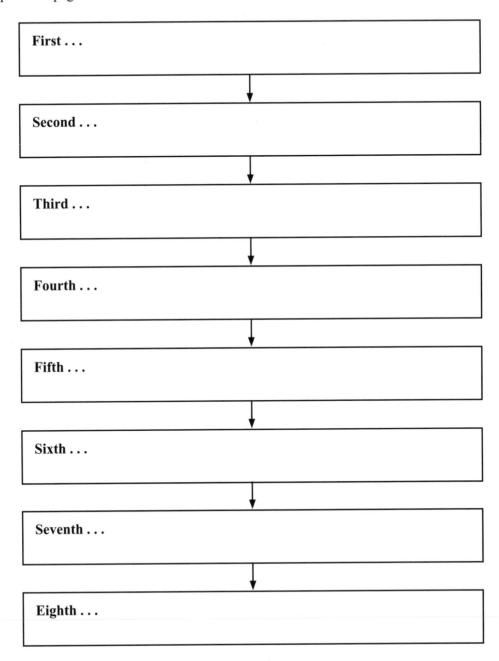

First . . .

Second . . .

Third . . .

Fourth . . .

Fifth . . .

Sixth . . .

Seventh . . .

Eighth . . .

PERSUASIVE TECHNIQUES

Analyze five advertisements on television or the radio in order to determine the persuasive techniques that are being used. Place checks in the boxes to show which products use which persuasive techniques.

Product Advertised	Bandwagon	Testimonial	Broad Terms	Negativity	Emotional Appeal

PERSUASIVE TOPICS

A persuasive paper uses facts and statistics to convince the reader of an opinion or to take some sort of action. It is not objective, like a descriptive paper. In a persuasive paper, the writer definitely takes a side. Give a topic for a persuasive research paper for each of the given subjects.

1. Adoption

   _____

   _____

   _____

2. Tattoos and piercing

   _____

   _____

   _____

3. Elections

   _____

   _____

   _____

4. Health care

   _____

   _____

   _____

5. Animal rights

   _____

   _____

   _____

PERSUASION TABLE

Most persuasive papers consider two sides of an issue. A persuasion table will help you organize arguments for (*pro*) and against (*con*) the side you take. Complete the table below to plan a persuasive research paper. You can use a topic from the previous page.

For (Pro)	Against (Con)

PERSUASIVE PLANNER

Once you have completed a persuasion table, you can use a second organizer to arrange the information for your actual paper. Complete the planner below to plan a persuasive research paper. You can use a topic from the earlier page.

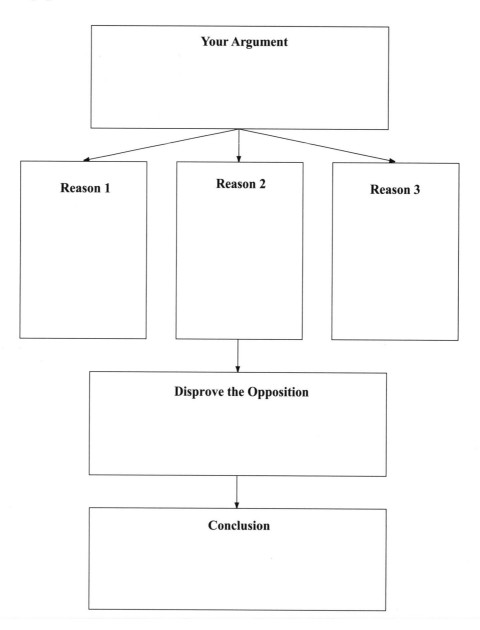

CAUSE-AND-EFFECT TOPICS

A cause-and-effect paper tells about something that happens (the *cause*) and what happens as a result (the *effect*). Give a topic for a cause-and-effect research paper for each of the given subjects.

1. The popularity of health clubs

   _____

   _____

   _____

2. The high cost of running for public office

   _____

   _____

   _____

3. The decline of musical theater

   _____

   _____

   _____

4. Single-parent households

   _____

   _____

   _____

5. The popularity of fast food restaurants

   _____

   _____

   _____

FISHTAIL GRAPH

In a *fishtail graph,* the "head" is a single cause or single effect. Then the "tail" will hold the many causes or many effects, and details about each. Keep the cause or causes on the left side of the page and the effect or effects on the right side. Complete the fishtail graph below to plan a cause-and-effect research paper. You can use a topic from the previous page.

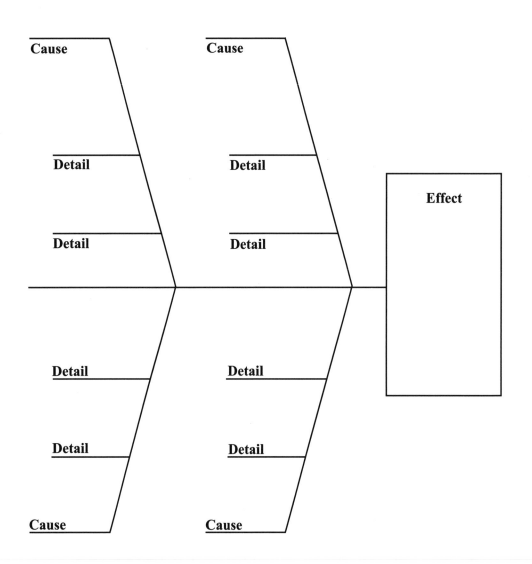

PROBLEM-AND-SOLUTION TOPICS

A problem-and-solution paper explains a problem and then offers a solution. Give a topic for a problem-and-solution research paper for each of the given subjects.

1. The cost of a college education

   _____

   _____

   _____

2. Neighborhood crime

   _____

   _____

   _____

3. Increased use of video games

   _____

   _____

   _____

4. Immigration

   _____

   _____

   _____

5. Pollution

   _____

   _____

   _____

PROBLEM-AND-SOLUTION ORGANIZER 1

If your chosen problem has only one good solution, then you can plan your paper using a simple organizer. Complete the organizer below to plan a problem-and-solution research paper for a problem that has only one solution. You can use a topic from the previous page.

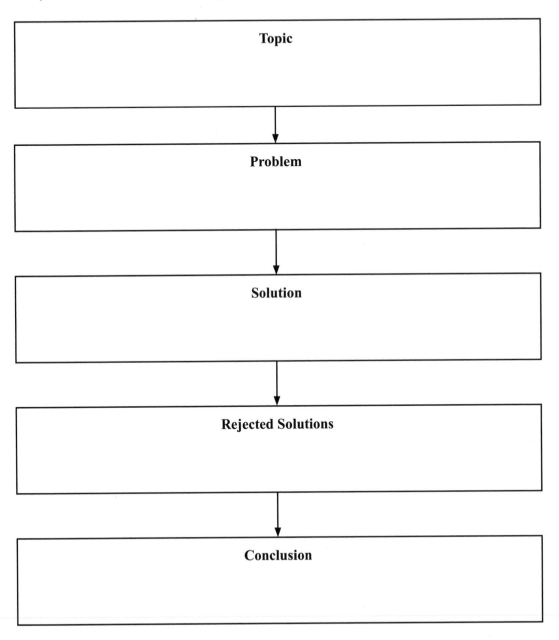

Topic

Problem

Solution

Rejected Solutions

Conclusion

PROBLEM-AND-SOLUTION ORGANIZER 2

If your chosen problem has more than one good solution, then you can plan your paper using a more complex organizer. Complete the organizer below to plan a problem-and-solution research paper for a problem that has more than one solution. You can use a topic from the earlier page.

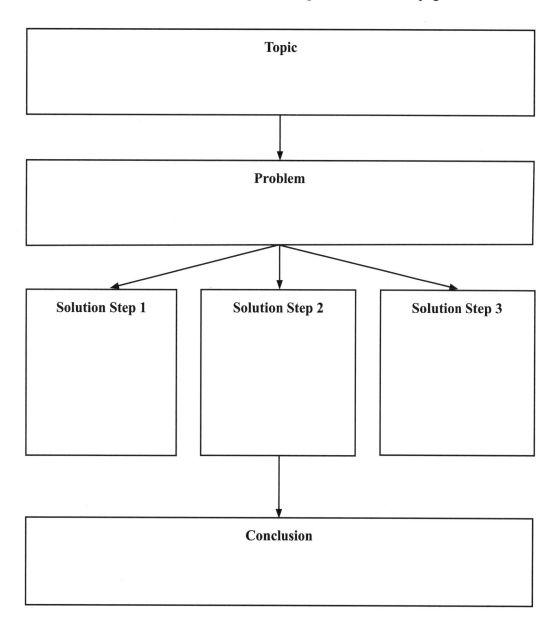

COMPARE-AND-CONTRAST TOPICS

A compare-and-contrast paper examines the similarities and differences of two things. Give a topic for a compare-and-contrast research paper for each of the given subjects.

1. Communism

   _____

   _____

   _____

2. Sports

   _____

   _____

   _____

3. Cultures

   _____

   _____

   _____

4. Soap operas

   _____

   _____

   _____

5. Music genres

   _____

   _____

   _____

VENN DIAGRAM

One of the best ways to get your ideas organized is to make a *Venn diagram*. In this diagram, you write things that are common between the two subjects in the area where the two circles overlap. The details that are different about the subjects are written in the sections of the circles that do not overlap. Complete the Venn diagram below to plan a compare-and-contrast research paper. You can use a topic from the previous page.

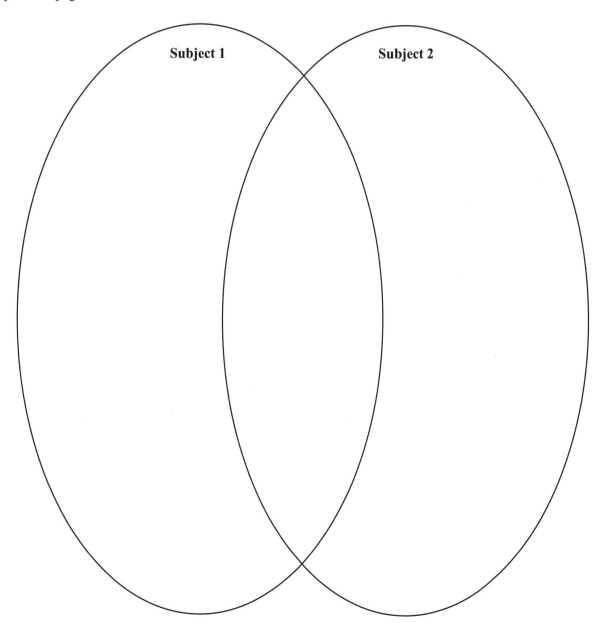

Subject 1   **Subject 2**

COMPARE-AND-CONTRAST TABLE

Writing your ideas on a table will also help you get your ideas organized. Complete the table below to plan a compare-and-contrast research paper. You can use a topic from the earlier page.

	Subject 1	Subject 2
Point A		
Point B		
Point C		
Point D		

TRANSITION SCRAMBLE

You can use transition words to transition from one idea or sentence to another. Using transition words and phrases will help your writing flow better. Unscramble the transition words below. Write the correct words in the spaces provided.

1. nayadiltoild _____

2. tgoluahh _____

3. dibsees _____

4. qclensentyou _____

5. ueaenvlylt _____

6. nayifll _____

7. ohveerw _____

8. aiiinllty _____

9. aimeenlhw _____

10. viperlousy _____

11. llsmiiray _____

12. ceins _____

13. ethofreer _____

14. ilunke _____

15. lhiew _____

SOURCE WORD SEARCH

Circle each of the terms in the puzzle.

ALMANAC	ENCYCLOPEDIA	NEWSPAPER
ALTAVISTA	GOOGLE	NONFICTION
ATLAS	HANDBOOK	ONLINE
BIOGRAPHICAL REFERENCE	INTERNET	PERIODICAL
BOOLEAN	JOURNAL	REFERENCE BOOK
CUTTER NUMBER	KEYWORD	RELIABLE
DEWEY DECIMAL SYSTEM	LIBRARY	SEARCH ENGINE
DICTIONARY	MAGAZINE	YAHOO
DOGPILE	METASEARCH	

A	L	A	N	R	U	O	J	B	I	E	R	N	E	W	S	P	A	P	E	R
B	I	O	G	R	A	P	H	I	C	A	L	R	E	F	E	R	E	N	C	E
Y	B	S	E	A	R	C	H	E	N	G	I	N	E	Z	E	D	N	I	T	B
O	R	I	C	A	I	O	N	C	A	E	E	A	N	H	N	M	A	L	C	M
C	A	N	A	M	L	A	A	P	E	N	M	L	C	W	I	U	E	K	A	U
O	R	R	Y	Y	D	T	S	Y	I	L	T	L	Y	Y	Z	N	L	R	T	N
A	Y	Y	D	E	R	W	A	Z	A	E	O	N	C	E	A	R	O	I	A	R
E	M	L	V	L	E	A	A	V	M	R	O	P	L	K	G	O	O	G	L	E
E	L	L	T	N	R	T	N	E	I	I	E	T	O	I	A	T	B	A	E	T
R	E	L	I	A	B	L	E	O	T	S	A	M	P	A	M	T	Y	L	H	T
P	B	O	A	M	V	A	O	C	I	N	T	A	E	R	E	U	I	Y	R	U
I	E	E	T	C	A	S	I	O	T	T	C	A	D	A	N	P	N	R	I	C
G	U	R	N	E	I	F	S	U	L	E	C	B	I	O	G	E	T	N	E	E
N	N	E	I	L	N	D	L	T	Y	N	H	I	A	O	N	E	E	L	N	D
E	R	K	O	O	B	D	N	A	H	I	N	L	D	O	B	E	R	R	U	R
H	E	S	N	N	D	N	N	I	R	L	Y	L	I	H	Y	D	N	C	I	O
C	T	Y	E	R	A	I	R	Y	R	N	G	T	E	A	C	T	E	F	R	W
R	E	F	E	R	E	N	C	E	B	O	O	K	K	Y	N	I	T	A	A	Y
E	M	E	T	S	Y	S	L	A	M	I	C	E	D	Y	E	W	E	D	H	E
S	C	A	U	J	H	H	L	S	L	M	E	T	A	S	E	A	R	C	H	K

THE DEWEY DECIMAL SYSTEM

The Dewey decimal system is a way to classify books. The system is based on ten classes of subject (000–999), which are then divided into subjects that are more specific. Fill in the blanks. For some you will need to give the category number. For others you will fill in the category name.

	Class Number	Class Name
1.		Natural Sciences and Mathematics
2.		Social Sciences
3.	100s	
4.		Literature and Rhetoric
5.		Religion
6.	900s	
7.	700s	
8.		Technology and Applied Sciences
9.	400s	
10.	000s	

LIBRARY EXPLORATION ACTIVITY

Each of the ten main classes of the Dewey decimal system has its own number. Write down the titles, authors, and call numbers of two books from each class of the Dewey decimal system.

000 General Works

Title: _____ Author: _____ Call Number: _____

_____

_____

100 Philosophy and Psychology

Title: _____ Author: _____ Call Number: _____

_____

_____

200 Religion

Title: _____ Author: _____ Call Number: _____

_____

_____

300 Social Sciences

Title: _____ Author: _____ Call Number: _____

_____

_____

400 Language

Title: _____ Author: _____ Call Number: _____

_____

_____

500 Natural Sciences and Mathematics

Title: _____ Author: _____ Call Number: _____

_____

_____

600 Technology and Applied Sciences

Title: _____ Author: _____ Call Number: _____

_____

_____

700 Fine Arts

Title: _____ Author: _____ Call Number: _____

_____

_____

800 Literature

Title: _____ Author: _____ Call Number: _____

_____

_____

900 Geography and History

Title: _____ Author: _____ Call Number: _____

_____

_____

REFERENCE BOOKS

Reference books include encyclopedias, dictionaries, almanacs, and many other specialty books. Match the type of reference book with the correct description and write the correct letters in the left-hand column.

Type	Description
_____ 1. Almanac	a) a work that provides information about a person's life (education, accomplishments, awards, career, etc.)
_____ 2. Atlas	b) a book of maps and geographical information
_____ 3. Biographical reference	c) a compilation of statistics and facts on a variety of subjects, usually in one volume
_____ 4. General encyclopedia	d) a book that provides words and definitions devoted to one field of study
_____ 5. Handbook	e) a work meant to provide comprehensive summaries of all fields of knowledge or specific branches of knowledge
_____ 6. Specialized dictionary	f) concise—but usually comprehensive— explanatory facts, figures, and statistics, usually in multiple volumes per year

PERIODICALS SEARCH

Periodicals are published on a regular basis, often dozens or hundreds of times per year. The most common types of periodicals you will use are journals, magazines, and newspapers. Use resources at the library to find a periodical for each of the following areas. Write the name of the periodical in the space provided.

Art _____

Business _____

Communications _____

Computers _____

Crafts _____

Criminal Justice _____

Education _____

History _____

Literature and Language _____

Mathematics _____

Music _____

Nursing _____

Political Science _____

Psychology _____

Public Relations _____

Science _____

Social Work _____

Sociology _____

INTERNET SCAVENGER HUNT

Complete the activity below using the Internet and available search engines.

1. What is the first line of the Beatles song, "Ticket to Ride"?

   Answer: _____

   Search engine used: _____

   Search terms used: _____

   Number of searches needed to find the answer: _____

2. Find a recipe for apple pie that MUST include cinnamon and nutmeg.

   Name of recipe: _____

   Search engine used: _____

   Search terms used: _____

   Number of searches needed to find the answer: _____

3. Who was the Italian to first put the numerical scale on the thermometer?

   Answer: _____

   Search engine used: _____

   Search terms used: _____

   Number of searches needed to find the answer: _____

4. Who was the first African–American woman to win an Academy Award?

Answer: _____

Search engine used: _____

Search terms used: _____

Number of searches needed to find the answer: _____

5. What is the highest point in the continental U.S. (i.e., the lower 48 states)?

Answer: _____

Search engine used: _____

Search terms used: _____

Number of searches needed to find the answer: _____

6. Who invented aluminum foil?

Answer: _____

Search engine used: _____

Search terms used: _____

Number of searches needed to find the answer: _____

SUCCESSFUL SEARCHES

It's important to know the best way to search for something on the Internet. Not only do you need to know the best search engine to use, you have to choose the right keywords. Choose the best answer for each question.

1. If you wanted to find pages with haiku poems about orchids, which of the following queries would be the most useful?

   a) +Haiku +Orchid
   b) +haiku +Orchid
   c) +haiku +orchid
   d) haiku orchid

2. If you typed the unusual expression below into a search engine, which of them would result in finding the FEWEST sites?

   a) Carla's wig
   b) "Carla's wig"
   c) +Carla +wig
   d) +carla +wig

3. Suppose you were interested in finding a statue of Venus, the Roman goddess of Love. Which search would get you there best?

   a) +Venus +goddess –planet +statue
   b) +Venus +goddess +planet +statue
   c) Venus goddess planet statue
   d) +Ven* +goddess –planet +statue

RELIABLE WEBSITE CHECKLIST

When considering using a website as a source, use the checklist below to ensure that your Internet sources are reliable for research.

☐ Who wrote the web page, and what is his or her background?

☐ What is the contact information for the author?

☐ What is the business or organization that is behind this website?

☐ Why did the author create this web page?

☐ How up-to-date is the information on the web page?

☐ Is the information objective?

INTERVIEW CHECKLIST

Sometimes you won't find the information you need for your report in the library. Look for a local expert who knows all about the topic you're researching. You may be able to interview this expert to get the information you need for your research paper. Use the checklist below to ensure you conduct a quality interview.

☐   Contact the expert and arrange the interview about a week in advance.

☐   Use a tape recorder.

☐   If possible, give the expert your questions in advance.

☐   Prepare a list of questions, but be flexible.

☐   Confirm your appointment, be well dressed, and be on time.

☐   During the interview, give the expert time to think. Take careful notes, and listen, listen, listen.

☐   At the end of the interview, give the expert your name and phone number, and thank him or her for taking the time to meet with you.

☐   Write a thank-you note within 24 hours.

CROSSWORD PUZZLE

Use the clues to complete the puzzle.

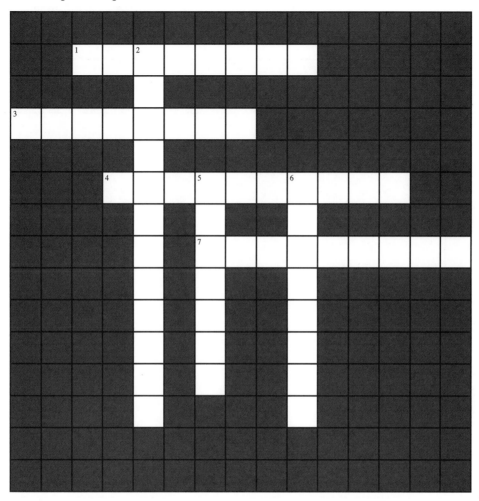

Down

2. paragraph that is at the beginning of a book or article
5. the words that accompany a picture, graph, or illustration
6. reading to find specific information

Across

1. topic of a paragraph (2 words)
3. major sections that books are divided into
4. paragraph that is at the end of a book or article
7. a collection of sentences with one main idea

DOCUMENTATION OPTIONS

It is critical that you keep track of the information you find in your research so that you can find what you need later when you begin to write. Write the benefits and drawbacks of each way to document the information you find as you research sources.

	Benefits	Drawbacks
Photocopies		
Note cards		
Computer		

SOURCE CARDS

You can create source cards to keep track of the sources used in your research. Label the parts of source cards for both print and web sources.

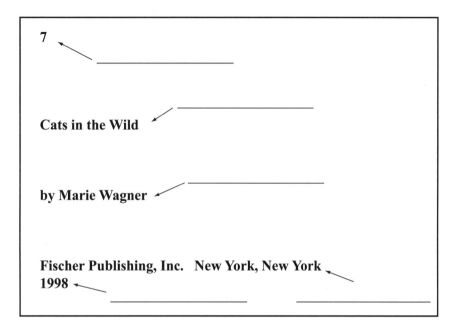

7 _____

Cats in the Wild _____

by Marie Wagner _____

Fischer Publishing, Inc.   New York, New York _____
1998 _____
_____   _____

3 _____

"Cats in the Wild" _____

http://www.cartoon-house.com/bios/schutz
Cartoon House, West Nyack, New York
Copyright 2005 _____
_____

NOTE CARDS

Creating note cards of your research will help you stay organized. Note cards include a summary of your research so that you can later group your cards by topic, making it easier to write your paper. Label the parts of a note card.

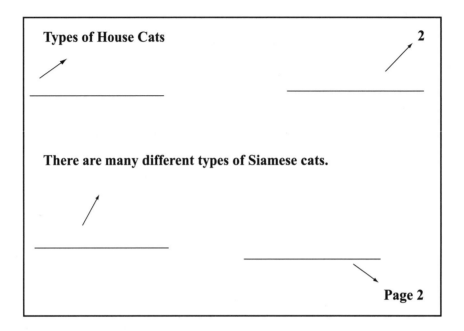

ACCURACY

The first way to evaluate a source is to determine if it is accurate. In other words, does the information seem correct? Use the space below to describe how you would evaluate a resource for accuracy.

1. _____

_____

_____

_____

_____

_____

2. _____

_____

_____

_____

_____

_____

3. _____

_____

_____

_____

_____

_____

EXPERT OPINIONS

When you are researching, an author may express an opinion on a given topic. In these instances, you need to consider the author. Is he or she an expert? An expert will have credentials, or documentation showing that he or she has experience in the area. Use the space below to describe how you would evaluate an expert opinion.

_____

_____

_____

_____

_____

_____

_____

_____

_____

_____

_____

_____

_____

_____

_____

_____

_____

_____

_____

_____

BIAS

Information you use in your research should be objective. The author should not have an unfair interest in the information he or she writes about. The information should be fair, not biased. Use the space below to describe how you would evaluate a resource for bias.

_____

_____

_____

_____

_____

_____

_____

_____

_____

_____

_____

_____

_____

_____

_____

_____

_____

_____

_____

_____

VARIETY

It is important to get information from many different sources. If you use information from only one author for your entire paper, your teacher will look at your research as incomplete. Use the space below to describe how you would evaluate your sources for variety.

_____

_____

_____

_____

_____

_____

_____

_____

_____

_____

_____

_____

_____

_____

_____

_____

_____

_____

_____

_____

_____

CURRENCY

When you do your research, you need to look at how recent the information is. Use the space below to describe how you would evaluate a resource for currency.

_____

_____

_____

_____

_____

_____

_____

_____

_____

_____

_____

_____

_____

_____

_____

_____

_____

_____

_____

_____

EVALUATING WEB SOURCES

Before you assume that a website is an appropriate source for your research, you must evaluate it like you would any source. Additionally, for these Internet sources, there are a few other points to consider. Answer the questions below.

1. How can the type of website (.com, .net, .org, .gov) help you decide how reliable the information on a website is?

_____

_____

_____

_____

_____

_____

_____

2. What should you look out for when using college websites to do your research?

_____

_____

_____

_____

_____

_____

_____

3. How would you evaluate a website for bias?

_____

_____

_____

_____

_____

_____

4. How would you evaluate a website for accuracy?

_____

_____

_____

_____

_____

_____

5. How would you evaluate a website for expert opinion?

_____

_____

_____

_____

_____

_____

NOTE CARD TOPICS

If you gathered and documented your research on note cards, then you can take that system a step further to organize your paper. The topics you wrote on the top of the cards can also be used to structure your essay. Those headings also show you related information that you can group together, and you can see how all your information might be ordered within the essay. Write the topics that you have found for your note cards in the following boxes. Write them in the order that you will organize your paper. You do not need to use every box.

NOTE CARD ORGANIZATION

Write the topics and ideas that you have found for your note cards in the following boxes. Write the ideas for each topic in the order in which you will write. You do not need to use every box.

Topic 1: _____

- _____
- _____
- _____
- _____
- _____
- _____
- _____

Topic 2: _____

- _____
- _____
- _____
- _____
- _____
- _____
- _____

Topic 3: _____

- _____
- _____
- _____
- _____
- _____
- _____
- _____

Topic 4: _____

- _____
- _____
- _____
- _____
- _____
- _____
- _____

Topic 5: _____

- _____
- _____
- _____
- _____
- _____
- _____
- _____

Topic 6: _____

- _____
- _____
- _____
- _____
- _____
- _____
- _____

Topic 7: _____

- _____
- _____
- _____
- _____
- _____
- _____
- _____

Topic 8: _____

- _____
- _____
- _____
- _____
- _____
- _____
- _____

TREES

Trees are a way to show the logic behind the information in your paper. You can make a tree with note cards, you can build it with self-stick notes, or you can draw it on a large sheet of paper. Trees are great organizational tools. Use the tree below to organize the ideas you found in your research.

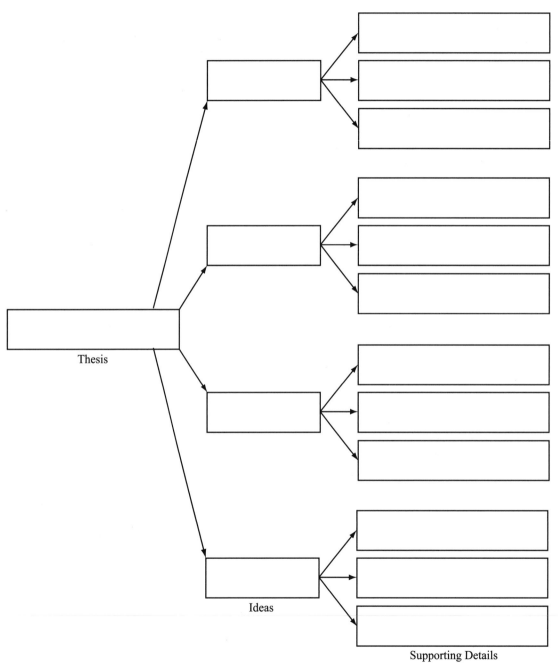

Thesis

Ideas

Supporting Details

TREE CHECKLIST

Your teacher might require that you turn in an outline before your paper is due. This is pretty common, especially for your first paper for that teacher. This allows him or her to check your ideas and offer suggestions. If you use a tree to organize your ideas, use this checklist before you submit your outline to your teacher to be sure that your ideas are organized properly.

☐   All of the branches tell something about the thesis.

☐   Each idea has at least two supporting details.

☐   Each part of the tree is a complete thought or sentence.

☐   Ideas do not repeat from one branch to another.

ROMAN NUMERAL REFRESHER

You'll need to be familiar with Roman numerals to write your outlines. Write the missing number below. The first one is done for you.

1. 19 = _____XIX_____

2. XIII = _____

3. XV = _____

4. XXX = _____

5. IX = _____

6. VII = _____

7. 26 = _____

8. VI = _____

9. XXXI = _____

10. XI = _____

11. 1 = _____

12. XX = _____

13. XIV = _____

14. IV = _____

15. 17 = _____

16. XVIII = _____

17. VIII = _____

18. II = _____

19. 12 = _____

20. X = _____

21. 3 = _____

22. XXIV = _____

23. XXIX = _____

24. XXV = _____

25. 27 = _____

26. XVI = _____

27. XXVIII = _____

28. V = _____

29. XXII = _____

30. XXI = _____

UNDERSTANDING OUTLINE LEVELS

The logic in an outline tells you that if you list an *A*, you have to at least list a *B*. For every *1*, there must be a *2*. Think of it this way: If you were giving your mom reasons why you should be able to go to the mall, you wouldn't say, "First, I need new clothes," then never give a second reason. It's the same with outlines. For each level you start with a *I, A, 1, a,* and so on, you have to give at least one other piece of information at the same level. Complete the outline by writing in the missing numbers or letters.

I.

_____

    1.

      a.

        (1)

          (a)

          _____

        _____

          _____

          (b)

      b.

        _____

        (2)

     _____

      _____

      b.

   _____

  _____

   _____

  B.

OUTLINE YOUR RESEARCH

Use the outline below to organize your ideas and research. Remember to include your thesis statement at the beginning, and take the time to carefully craft your arrangement of ideas.

I. Introduction _____

_____

_____

_____

_____

II. Body _____

    A. Point 1 Main Idea: _____

        1. Supporting Point #1 _____

        _____

        2. Evidence for Supporting Point #1 _____

        _____

    B. Point 2 Main Idea: _____

        1. Supporting Point #2 _____

        _____

        2. Evidence for Supporting Point #2 _____

        _____

C. Point 3 Main Idea: _____

    1. Supporting Point #3 _____

    _____

    2. Evidence for Supporting Point #3 _____

    _____

D. Point 4 Main Idea: _____

    1. Supporting Point #4 _____

    _____

    2. Evidence for Supporting Point #4 _____

    _____

E. Point 5 Main Idea: _____

    1. Supporting Point #5 _____

    _____

    2. Evidence for Supporting Point #5 _____

    _____

III. Conclusion _____

_____

_____

_____

_____

_____

THE UNUSUAL FACT INTRODUCTION

When starting the introduction to your research paper, you have some flexibility in how you can begin. The key is to start in a way that makes the reader want to find out more. Use the writing frame below to write your introduction using an unusual fact from your research.

Unusual fact

_____

_____

_____

_____

_____

_____

_____

_____

_____

Sentence beginning to relate fact to thesis

_____

_____

_____

_____

_____

_____

_____

_____

_____

Sentence relating more closely to thesis

_____

_____

_____

_____

_____

_____

_____

_____

_____

Thesis statement

_____

_____

_____

_____

_____

_____

_____

_____

_____

THE INTERESTING QUOTATION INTRODUCTION

You can also begin your paper with an interesting quotation to draw in the reader. Use the writing frame below to write your introduction using an interesting quotation from your research.

Interesting quotation

_____

_____

_____

_____

_____

_____

_____

_____

_____

Sentence beginning to relate quote to thesis

_____

_____

_____

_____

_____

_____

_____

_____

_____

_____

_____

_____

_____

_____

_____

_____

_____

_____

Thesis
statement

_____

_____

_____

_____

_____

_____

_____

_____

_____

_____

THE IMPORTANT STATISTIC INTRODUCTION

Starting your paper with an important statistic will make you seem knowledgeable about your topic. Use the writing frame below to write your introduction using an important statistic from your research.

Important statistic

_____
_____
_____
_____
_____
_____
_____
_____
_____
_____

Sentence beginning to relate statistic to thesis

_____
_____
_____
_____
_____
_____
_____
_____
_____
_____

Sentence
relating more
closely
to thesis

_____
_____
_____
_____
_____
_____
_____
_____
_____
_____

Thesis
statement

_____
_____
_____
_____
_____
_____
_____
_____
_____
_____
_____
_____

THE QUESTION INTRODUCTION

Starting your paper with a question will get your reader thinking about the topic. Use the writing frame below to write your introduction using a question.

Question

_____

_____

_____

_____

_____

_____

_____

_____

_____

Sentence beginning to relate question to thesis

_____

_____

_____

_____

_____

_____

_____

_____

Sentence
relating more
closely
to thesis

_____

_____

_____

_____

_____

_____

_____

_____

_____

Thesis
statement

_____

_____

_____

_____

_____

_____

_____

_____

_____

QUALITY QUOTATIONS

Quotations need to be included in your writing in a subtle way. You can blend quotations into your writing by adding a few words to introduce the quote. Rewrite the paragraph below to better incorporate the quotation into the writing.

Carol Burke said, "We want our students to count on at least one healthy meal here at school." Burke is the nutritionist for Harris County schools. She trains the food service staff how to carefully select and measure portions of food. "We have also changed to lower fat food choices," she said.

_____

_____

_____

_____

_____

_____

_____

_____

_____

_____

_____

_____

_____

_____

_____

_____

_____

FINE FOCUS

Focus is what keeps you from going off-topic. Each paragraph should address only one idea—the idea given in the topic sentence. Rewrite the paragraph below to focus on the main idea.

> States have made laws to ensure school lunches are nutritious. Children can bring their lunches from home or purchase either a hot or cold lunch at Harris County schools. Parents are also asked to not send candy, sodas, or cakes for birthdays. Instead, they can send goody bags.

_____

_____

_____

_____

_____

_____

_____

_____

_____

_____

_____

_____

_____

_____

_____

_____

_____

DANDY DEVELOPMENT

Good development is a balance between giving enough information to be clear and not too much to be boring. Rewrite the paragraph below to show better development.

School lunches should have acceptable portions for the age of the students. Children should get protein, carbohydrates, vitamins, and minerals in every meal.

_____

_____

_____

_____

_____

_____

_____

_____

_____

_____

_____

_____

_____

_____

_____

_____

_____

CRYSTAL-CLEAR CLARITY

Your thoughts as a writer should be perfectly clear to the reader. You want to be sure that the reader knows exactly what you mean. Clarity comes from choosing clear, concise words, and writing enough of them. Rewrite the paragraph below to show better clarity.

The foods the school district purchases meet USDA guidelines. Vendors must meet minimum standards for vitamins and minerals. The fat content and amount of carbohydrates are strictly regulated.

_____

_____

_____

_____

_____

_____

_____

_____

_____

_____

_____

_____

_____

_____

_____

_____

TALENTED TECHNIQUE

There are two elements to having good writing technique. First, you should choose words that are vivid and engaging. Use as little passive voice as possible. The second part of technique is how well you design your sentences. Interesting reading has sentences that have different structures and length. Rewrite the paragraph below to show better technique.

Healthy eating is very important. Good food choices are available in the school cafeteria. There are delicious foods available too.

_____

_____

_____

_____

_____

_____

_____

_____

_____

_____

_____

_____

_____

_____

_____

_____

A POWERFUL CONCLUSION

Conclusions restate the thesis. Conclusions also emphasize your strongest arguments or ideas. Finally, conclusions give readers something to think about. Use the writing frame below to write your conclusion.

Thesis

_____
_____
_____
_____

Sentence beginning to relate thesis to your "So what?" factor

_____
_____
_____
_____

Sentence relating more closely to your "So what?" factor

_____
_____
_____
_____

Your "So what?" factor

_____
_____
_____

WEAK TITLES

It's important to give your research paper a title that explains concisely what your paper is about. Rewrite these weak titles to better describe the content of the papers.

Distance Education

Compares college courses taken in person and those taken over computer and television

New Title: _____

Changes in Work Environment

Discusses the benefits and drawbacks of companies allowing employees to work from home

New Title: _____

Democracy

Explains how French and American democratic governments are closely related

New Title: _____

Information and Censorship

Explores the use of filters on public library computers to limit access to questionable and offensive websites

New Title: _____

The Variety of Life

Outlines the history of variety stores in the United States, from individually-owned five-and-dimes to stores like Kmart and the major superstores like Walmart

New Title: _____

CORRECT THE TITLES

The titles below break the basic rules for how titles should be written. Write them correctly.

1. Education in the early Republic was very different.

   _____

2. "New England Federalism"

   _____

3. Trade With China In The Early Nineteenth Century

   _____

4. Causes of the civil war

   _____

5. Historic Preservation in the twentieth century

   _____

6. American pottery

   _____

7. "American Impressionism"

   _____

8. the Life of Mark Twain

   _____

PLAGIARISM

Plagiarism is when a person takes another writer's words or ideas and uses them as his or her own. Answer the following questions about plagiarism.

1. When you use the work of another writer, you must give credit to the author in all of the following cases EXCEPT when

   a) you use the exact words of the author, within quotation marks
   b) you use the exact ideas of the writer but change the wording
   c) you write your thoughts after reading the author's text
   d) you use the writer's examples

2. Circle the act that is considered plagiarism.

   a) Allowing a parent to revise your work
   b) Using the exact words of another writer, within quotation marks and with a footnote
   c) Turning in a paper that a friend wrote for the same class last year
   d) Allowing classmates in your peer review group to comment on your paper

3. Circle the statement that is true.

   a) Paraphrased ideas do not need to be cited.
   b) You should write footnotes or endnotes, but not both.
   c) You should write footnotes or a bibliography, but not both.
   d) If you pay for a paper, it is not plagiarism.

COMMON KNOWLEDGE OR NOT?

Common knowledge is general information that most people know. Circle whether the information for each item is common knowledge or not.

1. Women and minorities make up 52.7 percent of the workers in American businesses.

   common knowledge   not common knowledge

2. Mohandas Gandhi was a pioneer in the concept of mass civil disobedience.

   common knowledge   not common knowledge

3. The cheetah is the fastest-moving land animal.

   common knowledge   not common knowledge

4. Smoking kills more than 400,000 people every year in the United States.

   common knowledge   not common knowledge

5. Abraham Lincoln was the sixteenth president of the United States.

   common knowledge   not common knowledge

QUOTATION, PARAPHRASE, AND SUMMARY

Read the passage below. Use the information from the passage to write a sentence using a direct quotation, then a sentence using a paraphrase, and finally a sentence using a summary.

> The beginning of the year 1946 finds the United States strong and deservedly confident. We have a record of enormous achievements as a democratic society in solving problems and meeting opportunities as they developed. We find ourselves possessed of immeasurable advantages— vast and varied natural resources; great plants, institutions, and other facilities; unsurpassed technological and managerial skills; an alert, resourceful, and able citizenry. We have in the United States Government rich resources in information, perspective, and facilities for doing whatever may be found necessary to do in giving support and form to the widespread and diversified efforts of all our people.
>
> —(Excerpted from *The State of the Union Address* [1946] by President Harry S. Truman)

Quotation: _____

_____

_____

_____

Paraphrase: _____

_____

_____

_____

Summary: _____

_____

_____

_____

FOOTNOTE AND ENDNOTE FORM

Footnotes and endnotes give credit to the writer whose words or ideas you used in your paper. A footnote is a note at the bottom of the page that tells where your information came from. Endnotes give the same information, but they are listed at the very end of the paper rather than on the page that the information appears. Label the format and punctuation of the note below.

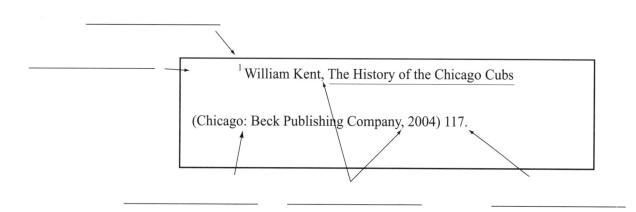

Label the parts of the note below.

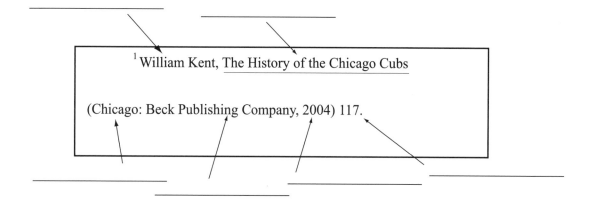

FOOTNOTES

Find a book, a newspaper, an encyclopedia, and a website on the same topic. Choose a quotation from each and find the correct information for the footnote.

Book

Name of book: _____

Name of author: _____

City of publisher: _____

Publisher: _____

Date of publication: _____

Page number: _____

Write the appropriate footnote for this quotation: _____

_____

Newspaper

Name of newspaper: _____

Date of newspaper: _____

Title of article: _____

Name of author (if available): _____

City of publication (if not part of newspaper name): _____

Page number: _____

Write the appropriate footnote for this quotation: _____

_____

Encyclopedia

Name of encyclopedia: _____

Edition of encyclopedia: _____

Topic heading: _____

Author of topic information (if available): _____

City of publisher: _____

Publisher: _____

Date of publication: _____

Page number: _____

Write the appropriate footnote for this quotation: _____

_____

Website

Author of article (if available): _____

Title of document (if available): _____

Title of website: _____

Site path (http): _____

Date site was copyrighted (if available): _____

Date site was accessed: _____

Write the appropriate footnote for this quotation: _____

_____

BIBLIOGRAPHY

Find a book, a newspaper, an encyclopedia, and a website on the same topic. Find the correct information from each to cite the source in a bibliography.

Book

Name of book: _____

Name of author: _____

City of publisher: _____

Publisher: _____

Date of publication: _____

Write the appropriate bibliography for this source: _____

Newspaper

Name of newspaper: _____

Date of newspaper: _____

Title of article: _____

Name of author (if available): _____

City of publication (if not part of newspaper name): _____

Page number: _____

Write the appropriate bibliography for this source: _____

Encyclopedia

Name of encyclopedia: _____

Edition of encyclopedia: _____

Topic heading: _____

Author of topic information (if available): _____

City of publisher: _____

Publisher: _____

Date of publication: _____

Write the appropriate bibliography for this source: _____

Website

Author of article (if available): _____

Title of document (if available): _____

Title of website: _____

Site path (http): _____

Date site was copyrighted (if available): _____

Date site was accessed: _____

Write the appropriate bibliography for this source: _____

BIBLIOGRAPHY FORM

The bibliography credits all of your sources used for researching and writing your paper. Label the format and punctuation of the bibliographic citation below.

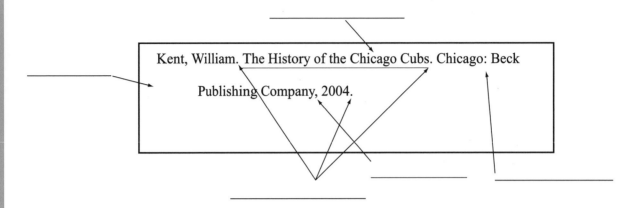

Kent, William. The History of the Chicago Cubs. Chicago: Beck

Publishing Company, 2004.

Label the parts of the bibliographic citation below.

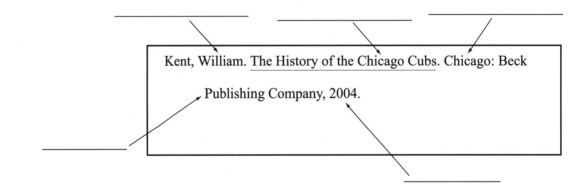

Kent, William. The History of the Chicago Cubs. Chicago: Beck

Publishing Company, 2004.

WORD SEARCH

Find each word in the puzzle and circle it.

CITATION	INDENT	SOURCES
COMMON KNOWLEDGE	PARAPHRASE	STYLE
ENDNOTE	PLAGIARISM	SUMMARIZE
FOOTNOTE	QUOTATION	SUPERSCRIPT

C	K	O	Q	I	L	S	O	X	A	N	W	W	Q	K	F	X	O	R	O
P	O	K	O	C	D	A	M	A	D	Q	X	D	B	H	V	B	O	J	C
C	E	M	O	P	I	H	B	N	Z	V	P	H	W	H	B	F	K	F	X
D	N	I	M	K	L	O	N	O	I	T	A	T	I	C	R	E	U	S	R
X	S	V	B	O	C	P	G	I	Z	J	R	C	Y	A	H	K	Y	T	Q
V	A	Q	C	B	N	M	L	T	D	H	A	Q	P	L	P	I	P	Y	M
N	U	G	R	C	U	K	D	A	O	B	P	J	G	T	T	I	N	N	H
P	Y	M	V	U	F	I	N	T	G	O	H	S	O	U	R	C	E	S	C
B	S	B	C	X	A	O	K	O	V	I	R	C	I	C	N	L	S	L	O
J	U	Q	N	U	R	S	P	U	W	H	A	M	S	R	I	T	W	A	G
S	E	G	R	Y	K	E	K	Q	M	L	S	R	P	B	H	D	J	I	H
Y	U	N	R	H	L	P	J	O	B	C	E	Z	I	R	A	M	M	U	S
F	D	A	E	A	X	Q	T	L	S	P	T	D	E	S	E	L	Q	G	L
K	U	A	Q	Q	A	V	F	G	U	L	O	E	G	N	M	I	K	S	J
E	A	N	E	Y	S	G	Q	S	Q	O	N	Q	D	E	W	F	I	C	O
Y	A	Q	G	H	A	T	U	M	P	D	T	N	E	D	N	I	T	C	P
V	M	J	J	H	Y	F	Y	F	I	L	O	D	M	T	V	I	W	T	R
E	F	F	X	C	C	E	O	L	Y	T	O	O	Y	Y	S	O	H	F	G
J	W	S	I	M	V	E	A	L	E	Z	F	Q	F	J	V	W	Q	C	A
D	O	K	E	Y	N	O	T	G	R	Z	F	X	Q	M	Q	E	S	E	R

CAPITALIZATION

Rewrite each sentence with the correct capitalization.

1. please don't bother me because i've had a hard day.

   _____

2. *to kill a mockingbird* was set in the town of maycomb, alabama.

   _____

3. paula and i are going to study thursday night for the big test in history.

   _____

4. the war of 1812 ended on saturday, december 24, 1814.

   _____

5. when you go to the store, please get some purina puppy chow.

   _____

6. the pool will open for the summer on saturday.

   _____

7. "we can have a city-wide picnic on labor day," mayor white suggested.

   _____

8. will you sign up to work at the spring fling?

   _____

9. we are visiting the navajo indian reservation.

   _____

10. we are reading a book about mother teresa.

    _____

11. there was a huge fire in yellowstone national park.

    _____

12. the painted desert has many beautiful colors.

    _____

13. don't think i'll let you get away with that!

_____

14. wednesday was named for woden, the norse god of war.

_____

15. easter is always on sunday.

_____

16. my hamsters are named sugarfoot and raisin.

_____

17. our school supply list stated that we need mead notebook paper.

_____

18. i'd like you to meet professor timothy adams.

_____

19. we are taking a vacation to the west coast.

_____

20. he said, "we will be talking about the great depression."

_____

PUNCTUATION CROSSWORD

Use the clues to complete the puzzle.

Down

1. " " (2 words)
2. –
6. ? (2 words)
7. …
8. :
10. ( )

Across

3. .
4. '
5. ;
9. ! (2 words)
11. ,
12. -

APOSTROPHE FOR POSSESSIVES

Add an apostrophe to each sentence to make the possessive correct.

1. Long ago, people thought the worlds surface was flat.

   _____

2. The lamps switch is broken.

   _____

3. Georgias award is displayed in a frame.

   _____

4. Why did Matthews attitude change?

   _____

5. Who said the actors performance was bad?

   _____

6. Hawaiis volcanoes have been active recently.

   _____

7. We searched the quarrys rubble for arrowheads.

   _____

8. The schools playground now has picnic tables.

   _____

9. Six kittens were born to Marks pet cat.

   _____

10. Davids plan is to hire more painters to finish the job.

   _____

APOSTROPHES FOR CONTRACTIONS

Rewrite the sentences using contractions for the underlined words.

1. Although he promised to build the treehouse, <u>I will</u> probably have to.

   _____

2. Carla said that <u>we are</u> like family to her.

   _____

3. Since <u>there will</u> be more sales after Labor Day, I'll go shopping then.

   _____

4. I wonder <u>who is</u> making all the noise.

   _____

5. You <u>are not</u> going to stay out late tonight.

   _____

6. Sandra just <u>could not</u> stay away from the chocolate cakes.

   _____

7. <u>That will</u> be the best way to solve our problems.

   _____

8. You told me <u>you have</u> never been to the zoo.

   _____

9. "He <u>is not</u> the fastest runner," she said.

   _____

10. "We <u>did not</u> forget your birthday," the children said.

    _____

COMMAS IN A SERIES

Rewrite each sentence using commas.

1. My grandfather served in World War II the Korean War and the Vietnam War.

   _____

2. This week I am going to the dentist having dinner with Grace and taking the dog to the vet.

   _____

3. What are the capitals of Illinois Alabama and New Mexico?

   _____

4. Please choose a book sit down and read quietly until the bell rings.

   _____

5. We had pancakes eggs and bacon for breakfast this morning.

   _____

6. We haven't decided whether to fish see a movie or take a trip.

   _____

7. School her job and piano practice took up all of Gloria's time.

   _____

8. My mom sings jazz gospel and blues.

   _____

9. Would you like burgers pizza or pasta for dinner?

   _____

10. Darla is taking a trip to New York New Jersey and Connecticut.

   _____

COMMAS WITH ADJECTIVES, PHRASES, AND INTERRUPTERS

Rewrite each sentence using commas.

1. The house they say is haunted.

   _____

2. The field was a sunny green meadow!

   _____

3. Garfield was a grumpy annoying cat.

   _____

4. Bill looks peaceful when he is asleep doesn't he?

   _____

5. The tiny determined ant climbed the hill with the crumbs.

   _____

6. The stickers had fallen off the old dusty paper.

   _____

7. Since she was the last person in line she had to turn off the lights.

   _____

8. Before I meet with your boss please tell me a little bit about her.

   _____

9. To find all the treats the children looked in every hiding place.

   _____

10. The woodpecker however lost its nest in the storm.

    _____

COMMAS IN LOCATIONS AND DATES

Rewrite each sentence using commas.

1. Christopher Columbus and his men sailed from Lisbon Portugal.

   _____

2. Mardi Gras is celebrated in New Orleans Louisiana.

   _____

3. Danny has grandparents in Dublin Ireland.

   _____

4. The Museum of Modern Art is in New York City New York.

   _____

5. My daughter was born in Oslo Norway.

   _____

6. I am going to visit my grandmother on April 4 2007.

   _____

7. The hospital was dedicated on August 28 1965.

   _____

8. The baby was born on September 27 1996.

   _____

9. Massachusetts became a state on February 6 1788.

   _____

10. Apollo 11 lifted off on July 16 1969.

   _____

HYPHEN OR DASH?

Circle whether the missing punctuation should be a hyphen or a dash.

1. My memories of Dad _____ some of my strongest memories _____ inspire me.

    hyphen   dash

2. When they leave for the store _____ it will be about an hour _____ they'll call you.

    hyphen   dash

3. The three _____ week _____ old injury does not appear to be healing.

    hyphen   dash

4. Her first job _____ cleaning houses _____ was hard work.

    hyphen   dash

5. She has a deep _____ seated fear of speaking in public.

    hyphen   dash

6. The family enjoyed hand _____ turned ice cream.

    hyphen   dash

7. At that moment I was interested in just one thing _____ namely, my lunch.

    hyphen   dash

8. June left her cat _____ how she loved that cat _____ to her favorite niece.

    hyphen   dash

9. The secretary sent a reply _____ requested fax.

    hyphen   dash

10. Tom's house _____ he inherited it from his parents _____ is for sale.

    hyphen   dash

THIRD-PERSON VOICE

Pronouns are words that take the place of nouns. (Think of words like *I, we, he, she, it, you,* and *they.*) Change the pronoun(s) in each sentence so that it is written in third person.

1. We went to the beach to enjoy the ocean breezes.

   _____

2. You dropped your ice cream on the floor!

   _____

3. We should do a better job during our student council meetings.

   _____

4. I jumped into the swimming pool.

   _____

5. We were late for school this morning.

   _____

6. I would like to play basketball after school.

   _____

7. We always sit together at lunch.

   _____

8. You should read the book I just finished!

   _____

9. May I borrow a pencil?

   _____

10. I love going to the zoo and the aquarium.

    _____

PRONOUNS AND NUMBER

Pronouns should agree in number. Singular nouns are matched with singular pronouns. Plural nouns are matched with plural pronouns. Rewrite each sentence, fixing the underlined error.

1. Everybody knows that broccoli provides <u>their bodies</u> with vitamin C.

   _____

2. The gymnasts shocked <u>her</u> audience with their amazing moves.

   _____

3. Either the lady or her mother gave <u>their</u> permission to pick flowers.

   _____

4. The computer and the video game have made <u>its</u> mark on modern life.

   _____

5. Which member of the boys' track team will beat <u>their</u> old record?

   _____

6. The volunteers for the dance received praise for <u>his</u> work.

   _____

7. The dry cleaner restored my filthy pants to <u>its</u> original condition.

   _____

8. The puppy and his mother cry until <u>her</u> owner feeds them.

   _____

PRONOUNS AND PERSON

Correct the underlined error in the space provided.

_____ 1. If any guests need some aspirin after that loud concert, <u>you</u> should hurry before the entire bottle is gone.

_____ 2. Mr. Bentley spoke for 45 minutes before <u>I</u> finally sat down.

_____ 3. The ladies wished that <u>she</u> had bought a cup of coffee before the meeting.

_____ 4. The lecture was so boring that Cindy focused on keeping <u>your</u> eyes open.

_____ 5. Every piece of Debra's jewelry glittered in the light and accented <u>our</u> eyes.

_____ 6. Mike's ties are so colorful that <u>I</u> says they could hypnotize people.

_____ 7. The band members made a unanimous decision to use <u>your</u> bake sale funds to buy new uniforms.

_____ 8. Eli needed scissors, but <u>we</u> couldn't find them anywhere.

_____ 9. Oreo, my dog, will not give up his treat even if <u>he</u> ask politely.

_____ 10. The professors at the community college prepare <u>our</u> students to be good citizens and good employees.

PRONOUN REFERENCE PROBLEMS

Circle whether the underlined pronoun has a clear reference or not.

1. Truman's hair is so long that he needs to visit the barber before <u>his</u> interview.

    clear   unclear

2. Chris never gets nervous before making a speech in Mrs. Smith's class, so <u>he</u> gives terrific presentations.

    clear   unclear

3. Mrs. Owen told her neighbor Mary that <u>she</u> was going to take a vacation to Hawaii.

    clear   unclear

4. I need to write a letter to the *Beacon News* because <u>it</u> have canceled my favorite comic strip.

    clear   unclear

5. My neighbors' lawn is so overgrown that <u>they</u> are growing more weeds than grass.

    clear   unclear

6. Aunt Kay mentioned that there was a car accident down the street from the block party, and <u>that</u> really upset the family.

    clear   unclear

7. <u>It</u> said that shrimpers are catching small amounts of fish in today's paper.

    clear   unclear

8. Some say that Elvis is still alive, but <u>he</u> doesn't believe it.

    clear   unclear

9. Mom and Donna are going to the market, because <u>she</u> needs eggs.

    clear   unclear

10. Sarah washed and braided <u>her</u> hair before the party.

    clear   unclear

11. It's my mom's birthday and I'd like to bake cookies for <u>her</u>.

    clear   unclear

12. We're going to make vanilla and chocolate cupcakes for our friends, and <u>they're</u> going to be good!

    clear   unclear

13. Sheryl is happy because today is <u>her</u> birthday.

    clear   unclear

14. Billy wants to visit Jackson in Texas, but <u>he</u> doesn't know how he'll get there.

    clear   unclear

15. Buster and Fido played together all day, and now <u>they're</u> very tired.

    clear   unclear

16. Aunt June shops for her sons Robert and Sam, but <u>he</u> doesn't always like what she buys.

    clear   unclear

SUBJECTIVE AND OBJECTIVE PRONOUNS

Underline the correct word in parentheses.

1. The plan was unsuccessful for Wanda and (he, him).

2. A note was sent to Lexie and (we, us).

3. The board members and (they, them) held a meeting.

4. (We, Us) volunteers must watch what we say carefully.

5. Janey talked to (she, her) and her mother.

6. Amelia gave the message to (she, her) and her friend.

7. The work has just started for Carla and (they, them).

8. She and (I, me) will run the race.

9. For (he, him) and Penny, there was a lot to choose from.

10. The rest of the team and (he, him) went to the restaurant.

11. Give the recipes to their friends and (they, them).

12. Vince and (she, her) gave a speech on the Gulf War.

13. It was for (she, her) and Jackie.

14. (They, Them) worked hard on the presentation.

15. (We, Us) singers performed yesterday.

16. Don't do anything until you hear from Sandy and (we, us).

17. I gave (she, her) and Sampson permission to stay.

18. He and (I, me) are wondering what to do.

19. The teacher and (we, us) are on a field trip right now.

20. It was a great day for them and (we, us).

PAST, PRESENT, AND FUTURE TENSE VERBS

Fill in the blank with the correct past verb tense.

1. My friend and I always _____ (speak) Spanish together.

2. I _____ (fail) to do my homework last Monday.

3. Todd and Kelly _____ (marry) last fall.

4. I _____ (think) Seattle was an interesting city.

5. Sherrie _____ (run) the New York marathon last year.

Fill in the blank with the correct present verb tense.

6. Terry _____ (work) as a cook at a fast food restaurant.

7. Mom _____ (grow) flowers in our garden.

8. Bob and Sue _____ (have) a housewarming party.

9. I will _____ (call) my family tonight.

10. My friend _____ (shop) on Thursdays.

Fill in the blank with the correct future verb tense.

11. My sister _____ (knit) a red hat.

12. I wonder when you _____ (finish) your report.

13. Angus _____ (have) a brand-new car.

14. We _____ (eat) lunch after the baseball game.

15. Lance and Sandy _____ (purchase) a new house.

PERFECT VERBS

Fill in the blank with the correct past perfect, present perfect, or future perfect verb tense.

Past Perfect

1. I _____ (live) in Texas for many years.

2. She _____ (brush) her teeth.

3. We _____ (clean) the bathroom yesterday.

4. Your daughter _____ (learn) gymnastics.

Present Perfect

5. I _____ (wash) the dishes after every meal.

6. I _____ (work) on the computer today.

7. I _____ (finish) that paper I've been working on.

8. You _____ (ask) him a few times to mow the lawn.

Future Perfect

9. Troy's hands were dirty because he _____ (plant) flowers in the garden.

10. We _____ (wait) here since 2:00!

11. In two weeks, my family and I _____ (travel) to New York.

12. I _____ (start) to take college classes.

PAST AND PRESENT PARTICIPLES

Complete the table with past and present participles for the given verbs.

Verb	Past Participle Tense (add *was, were, have been,* or *has been*)	Present Participle Tense (add *am* or *are*)
to save	has been saved	are saving
to agitate		
to notch		
to delay		
to embarrass		
to cuddle		
to brace		
to jeer		
to persist		
to meter		
to gaze		
to heave		
to filter		
to lecture		
to ooze		

IRREGULAR VERBS

Choose the correct verb for each sentence below.

1. When Mom _____ her finger at us, we knew we were in trouble.

   a) shaked   b) shook   c) had shook

2. When Trent saw the sketch, he wished that he had _____ it.

   a) drawn   b) drawed   c) drew

3. After Ted _____ Nancy's reaction to his outfit, he realized that he had not made a good first impression.

   a) saw   b) had saw   c) seen

4. Jennifer _____ her first day of school getting lost in all of the similar hallways.

   a) spend   b) spended   c) spent

5. Ms. Ames _____ several deep breaths to keep from losing her temper.

   a) taked   b) took   c) tooked

6. Yesterday Mike _____ two apples in the refrigerator for a snack.

   a) leaved   b) leaft   c) left

7. The second baseman picked up the ball and _____ it to first base.

   a) through   b) throwed   c) threw

8. The watermelon _____ on the floor in an explosion of pulp and seeds.

   a) busted   b) bursted   c) burst

9. Jimmy failed to see the gum and leaves that _____ to his shoe as he walked.

   a) sticked   b) stuck   c) stucked

10. The antics _____ little trust in Louise, who was very nervous about flying.

   a) built   b) build   c) builded

11. Joy would have _____ the dirty job of cleaning the barbecue grill.

    a) began   b) begun   c) beginned

12. After losing electricity during a hurricane, the Gomez family _____ candles.

    a) lit   b) lited   c) litted

13. Noel had _____ to the supermarket for the week's groceries.

    a) gone   b) went   c) goed

14. The pig farm in the area _____ up the neighborhood.

    a) stinked   b) stunk   c) stanked

15. Whenever Mike _____ his airplane, he worried about running out of fuel.

    a) flied   b) flown   c) flew

16. Amy had just _____ into her first forkful of omelet when she noticed bacon in it.

    a) bited   b) bitt   c) bitten

17. Maria _____ from the cold glass of water, trying to cool off from the heat of the day.

    a) drinked   b) drank   c) drunk

18. Randy would have _____ jeans and a T-shirt to the interview if he thought it would get him the job.

    a) wore   b) wored   c) worn

19. At first, Ramona _____ to tolerate Samuel's tardiness.

    a) chose   b) choose   c) choosed

20. One spring, Joe _____ tomatoes in the backyard instead of buying them from the store.

    a) grew   b) had grew   c) growed

SIMPLE SUBJECT-VERB AGREEMENT

A common problem writers run into is subject-verb agreement. For simple sentences, making the subject and verb agree usually is pretty simple. Circle the verb that agrees with the subject.

1. Ecologists are worried that some species of frogs **seems/seem** to be genetically changing.

2. Neither the coach nor the hitter **want/wants** to run the drill again.

3. Will they decide whether that group of travelers **boards/board** the plane before everyone?

4. Kimberly is the only one of the executives who **believe/believes** her project will succeed.

5. The cats in the shelter don't **belong/belongs** to you.

6. The media **is/are** not helping the situation with its articles.

7. Janet is one of those actresses who **audition/auditions** for roles that are too young for her.

8. The student body **hope/hopes** to raise enough money to pay for a scholarship.

9. Finding singers **has/have** been the job of the show's producers.

10. Sherri and Dave don't **knows/know** who has the map.

11. Megan and Charlie don't **understand/understands** today's math homework.

12. Beating Rico at tennis **is/are** impossible.

13. Those dogs shouldn't **play/plays** so rough!

14. Those dresses at the mall **is/are** perfect for the dance.

15. The large group of tourists **want/wants** to stop for lunch.

16. Amy and Loira **love/loves** to spend an afternoon watching scary movies.

17. He **cook/cooks** Thanksgiving dinner for the whole family.

18. Ralph can **fix/fixes** anything that's broken.

19. The whole class **cheer/cheers** when Ms. Lupo announces the party.

20. Raina **wonder/wonders** if she'll get a part in the school play.

SENTENCE FRAGMENTS

Writers sometimes write so fast they don't realize that their sentences are incomplete. These incomplete sentences are called *sentence fragments*. Read each short passage. Underline the part that is the sentence fragment.

1. Manny wasn't watching his plate very carefully. So Sissy, the family dachshund, grabbed a chicken leg hanging over the edge. As baked beans and potato salad slid onto Manny's new shoes.

2. Ever since Andrea peeked at Melinda's paper during the algebra quiz. She has been consumed by guilt. Even the grapes in her lunch seem like the accusing eyes of Ms. Gregson, her algebra teacher.

3. Jamie opened the door of his overfilled refrigerator. Which caused a package of berries to fall to the floor. The fruit bounced and rolled all over the kitchen floor.

4. Rita loves to walk her friends' dogs at Bellaire Park. For example, Kerry's poodle, Maizy, or Greta's collie, Kia. Lots of guys, Rita found, talk to girls with cute dogs.

5. Head down, Laura stared at the paper on her desk. She understood the sentence fragment that Mrs. Muniz was explaining. But was too shy to raise her hand and give an answer.

6. June found the pressure from her headache unbearable. Although she didn't want to leave in the middle of the lecture. She put her head in her hands.

7. Paulo left home early. To memorize the vocabulary for his science test. All that he could think about was getting to the library to meet his study group.

8. Chewing the dry, crumbly, rye toast bought at the health food store. Lorna tried to enjoy her snack. Dreaming about a cheesy piece of pizza didn't make the toast taste any better.

9. My dog Harley loves to sleep in odd places. Lately he prefers the rug under the kitchen table. Where his nose sniffs all around looking for crumbs that we might have dropped.

10. Bucking and rearing like a wild horse that cowboys had captured. The washer fought against its overfilled tub. On the other side of the laundromat, Buddy watched the TV, pretending that it was not his machine.

RUN-ON SENTENCES

Writers sometimes put too much information in a sentence by including more than one complete idea. When two or more sentences are written as one sentence, this is called a *run-on*. Correct each run-on sentence.

1. We bought shoes, clothes, towels, and swimsuits at the store fortunately, we have a large suitcase for the trip.

   _____

   _____

2. The young child seemed to be lost, she was crying and looking for her grandma.

   _____

   _____

3. My mother retired from the Army last year she is writing a book about her career.

   _____

   _____

4. Inspector Green came to our school he showed us some of his equipment and talked about the Treasury Department.

   _____

   _____

5. My nephew grew three inches in one year now he is much better at basketball.

   _____

   _____

6. I have to clean my room I have to make my bed before I catch the bus for school.

_____

_____

7. Marta wanted help with the recipe she couldn't make the dish alone.

_____

_____

8. We went to my cousin's wedding in Virginia over 300 people were at the reception.

_____

_____

9. Our baseball team won the tournament last week we had to go into extra innings to win.

_____

_____

10. Janelle's birthday is on October 6 she is going to the Fall Festival for her birthday celebration.

_____

_____

11. Kyla and Johnny worked very hard on their book report they felt they earned a better grade.

_____

_____

12. We will be on our annual trip to the shore next week we will not be able to attend the parade.

_____

_____

FREQUENTLY CONFUSED WORDS

Underline the correct word in parentheses.

1. Now (there, they're) shining with furniture polish, gleaming in the sunlight that pours through the window.

2. Cliff is so excited to buy his pizza for lunch today that he refused to (lose, loose) his place in line for the teacher.

3. The (weather, whether) is expected to change over the next few days.

4. She gave me a nice (complement, compliment) about my new haircut.

5. Oh, no! (There, Their) are kidney beans on my plate!

6. There are some (principals, principles) you have to understand to do well in geometry.

7. (Lay, Lie) the cookbook that I bought on the counter next to the flour canister.

8. I would go along on the nature hike except that it's (two, too) far for me to go.

9. Running (lose, loose) in the house, Gerry the Gerbil visited every room to see what she had been missing.

10. Not eating well, staying up late, and not doing the homework is bound to (effect, affect) your grade.

11. Do you know (whose, who's) writing folder was left in the computer lab?

12. If you turn (to, too) your left, you will see (two, too) birds building a nest.

13. (Its, It's) time to start planning the food for our family Thanksgiving celebration.

14. The campers put all of (their, they're) supplies and gear by the large cabin.

15. We had planned to see that new movie, but we can shop for some clothes (to, too).

16. If you need to speak to the counselors, (their, they're) in the large conference room.

17. (Your, You're) the only person we know who is capable of doing the job.

18. The cat at the animal shelter is larger (then, than) the puppy I have at home.

19. To prepare for the triathlon, I walked a mile; (then, than) I swam 40 laps at the pool.

20. I need to see if I can get a (dual, duel) degree in mathematics and molecular biology.

SPELLING SENTENCES

Underline the word with the correct spelling in parentheses.

1. Mom's (vacuum, vacum) cleaner is getting old and doesn't work very well.

2. There is a (vacancy, vacancie) in our apartment complex.

3. He was not (holy, wholly) convinced the boy was guilty.

4. His (sovereign, soveriegn) rights meant nothing to people from a democratic nation.

5. When you (shriek, shreik), the sound of your voice changes.

6. Please (specify, specefy) what ingredients you would like on your hamburger.

7. My sister is known to (vassilate, vacillate) over which outfit to wear each day.

8. Please (supress, suppress) your angry words until he has left the room.

9. Do we have (sufficient, sufficeint) water for our hike up the mountain?

10. Susan was (unskillful, unskillfull) at cooking.

11. The students stood at the (threshhold, threshold) of the door waiting for the bell to ring.

12. The (superintendant, superintendent) paid a cursory visit to our school.

13. So many (beautyiful, beautiful) flowers grow in our backyard.

14. Shirley made a (committment, commitment) to the school newspaper to act as editor.

15. It is not (all right, alright) to leave litter on the ground.

16. The teacher warned us that we would be (quizzed, quized) on today's lesson.

17. There is a (noticable, noticeable) change in Mr. Buford's appearance.

18. Milo got a part-time job working at a local (newstand, newsstand).

19. After the accident I was (sincerly, sincerely) sorry for what I had done.

20. The twins cut their hair so they would look (different, diffrent) from one another.

SPELLING CROSSWORD

Use the clues to complete the puzzle.

Across

5. the ability to be noticed

9. agreement of a group

10. the ability to pick out or discern

13. the ability to pass

15. a place where the dead are buried

16. levels of authority

17. jokingly, not serious

Down

1. the elected leader of a state

2. of whom the identity is unknown

3. very small

4. materials that are for sale in a store

6. youth, teenager

7. to see or understand

8. an infected growth

9. huge, enormous

11. the ability to change

12. an author of a play

14. to find not guilty

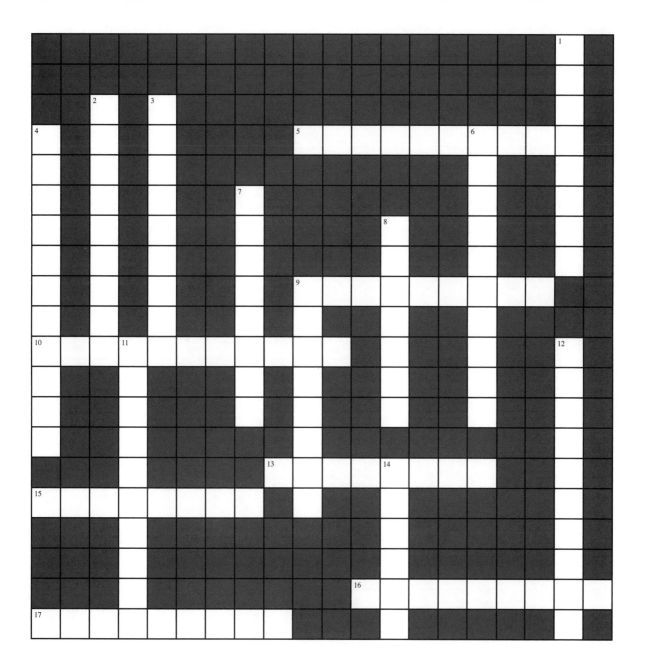

FEEDBACK WORKSHEET

Have someone read your paper and use the form to give feedback on your writing.

Editor: _____

Writer: _____

1. What is the thesis that the writer is trying to explain in the paper? If you cannot readily identify a thesis, suggest one (or more than one) based on the most interesting observations, ideas, and analysis in the paper.

    _____

    _____

    _____

    _____

    _____

    _____

2. Are there places where the paper drifts away from the thesis? Suggest ways to connect those sections to the thesis.

    _____

    _____

    _____

    _____

    _____

    _____

3. Find the interesting ideas in the paper that could be explained or developed more fully. Ask questions and make suggestions to help the writer.

    _____

    _____

    _____

    _____

    _____

4. Find the passages in the paper where the writer repeats material. Mark these passages on the paper, and make suggestions about how those parts could be eliminated.

    _____

    _____

    _____

    _____

    _____

5. Write a detailed note to the writer suggesting a plan for revision. (Use the back of the worksheet or additional paper if necessary.)

    _____

    _____

    _____

    _____

    _____

REVISION AND PROOFREADING CHECKLIST

Use the checklist as you revise your paper. Check off tasks as they are complete.

Content

☐ Does your title give a good idea of what your paper is about? Remember, "Research Paper" is not a good title!

☐ Is there an attention-getting introduction?

☐ Is your thesis statement clearly stated in the introduction?

☐ Does every paragraph have something to say about the thesis?

☐ Have you used enough examples to make your ideas clear?

☐ Have you avoided faulty reasoning in any argument?

☐ Does the conclusion give the reader something to think about?

Organization

☐ Does the organization match the type of paper you wrote?

☐ Can the reader clearly identify the introduction, body, and conclusion?

☐ Is your sequence logical?

☐ Do you use transition words to move from one idea to the next?

☐ Does each paragraph have information that is needed to explain or defend your thesis?

☐ Do you avoid introducing new information in your conclusion?

Research and Sources

☐ Do you use quotations, paraphrases, and summaries correctly?

☐ Are your footnotes/endnotes and bibliography in the style your teacher assigned?

☐ Are your sources authoritative?

☐ Is the research unbiased?

☐ Have you written your own comments for each piece of research included?

☐ Have you checked the direct quotations against the original source?

☐ Do quotations flow in the essay seamlessly?

☐ If material was paraphrased, are the sources included in the bibliography?

Style

☐ Do you use different verbs throughout the paper?

☐ Do you use too much passive voice?

☐ Do you use a variety of sentence structures and lengths?

☐ Is your choice of words clear and concise?

Proofreading

☐ Did you proofread on paper, using proofreader's marks to save time?

☐ Do all subjects and verbs agree?

☐ Are the verb tenses consistent?

☐ Are your sentences free of sentence fragments and run-ons?

☐ Do your pronouns agree with the words they substitute?

☐ Is all capitalization correct?

☐ Is all spelling correct?

☐ Are there any repeated words?

☐ Is all punctuation correct?

☐ Are the page numbers correct?

Teacher-Specific Checks

☐ Is the assignment complete?

☐ Do you use the margins, font, etc., that your teacher may have required?

☐ Is the information appropriate for the assignment?

ALTERNATIVE REVISION CHECKLIST

Use the checklist as you revise your paper. Check off tasks as they are complete.

I. Introduction

Yes	No	
☐	☐	Did you write a clear thesis?

II. Body

A. Topic One (the first reason/example why you believe your thesis)

Yes	No	
☐	☐	Does the first topic sentence support the thesis?
☐	☐	Do you explain each example and tell why it's important?
☐	☐	Are there enough examples, explanations, and details to provide support for the first topic sentence?
☐	☐	Do the examples and details follow a logical order?
☐	☐	Are the transition words used correctly?

B. Topic Two (the second reason/example why you believe your thesis)

Yes	No	
☐	☐	Did you use a transition to introduce your second topic?
☐	☐	Do you explain each example and tell why it's important?
☐	☐	Is this second topic sentence different from the first topic sentence?
☐	☐	Are there enough examples, explanations, and details to provide support for the second topic sentence?
☐	☐	Are these examples clearly different from the examples you used in your first topic?
☐	☐	Do the examples, details, and explanations (support) follow a logical order?
☐	☐	Are the transition words used correctly?

C. Topic Three (The third topic is only necessary if you need to provide additional support for your thesis.)

Yes	No	
☐	☐	Did you use a transition to introduce your third support topic?
☐	☐	Do you explain each example and tell why it's important?
☐	☐	Is your third topic sentence clearly different from your first and second topic sentences?
☐	☐	Are there enough examples, explanations, and details to provide support for the third topic sentence?
☐	☐	Are the examples clearly different from the examples you used in your first and second topic?
☐	☐	Do the examples, details, and explanations follow a logical order?
☐	☐	Are transition words used correctly?

III. Conclusion

Yes	No	
☐	☐	Did you restate the thesis?
☐	☐	Did you sum up your two or three topic sentences?
☐	☐	Did you give the reader something to think about?

IV. Overall Structure

Yes	No	
☐	☐	Does the whole essay flow in a logical order?
☐	☐	Is each paragraph related to the paragraph before it and the paragraph after it?
☐	☐	Do the introduction and conclusion discuss the thesis and supporting ideas?

V. Grammar

Yes	No	
☐	☐	Do your subjects and verbs agree?
☐	☐	Do your verbs follow a logical verb tense?
☐	☐	Do your pronouns match the nouns they are replacing? For example, students/they; Gallaudet/it; Carol/she; Bob/he.
☐	☐	Do you use capital letters where necessary? For example, proper nouns like English are always capitalized.
☐	☐	Do you use the correct choice of commonly confused words?
☐	☐	Is your spelling correct?

GRADING YOUR OWN PAPER

Use the following form to assess your own writing to determine your likely letter grade.

A–Excellent

An *A* essay includes all the characteristics of *B* and *C* work as well as the following:

_____ The writer offers an insightful thesis.

_____ The writer consistently offers clear and detailed explanations in support of the thesis.

_____ The reader has no doubt how the writer arrived at the conclusions offered.

_____ The sources are an integral part of the essay, incorporated smoothly into the flow of the writing.

_____ The essay is easy to read because it flows smoothly from idea to idea.

_____ There are few or no errors in grammar, mechanics, etc.

_____ The writer has made good use of language.

B–Good

A *B* essay includes all the characteristics of *C* work as well as the following:

_____ The writer has a more specific, focused thesis.

_____ The sources aren't just there but help to advance the argument.

_____ The writer consistently offers better explanation and support for the how and why of the definition.

_____ The paper is better organized, making good use of transitions and other signals to the reader about the direction of the essay.

C–Adequate or Competent

A *C* essay demonstrates the writer's ability to communicate ideas and has these characteristics:

_____ The writer has a clear thesis.

_____ The essay offers some explanation of how the writer arrived at the thesis.

_____ The essay offers some explanation of why the ideas are important to the writer.

_____ The essay is controlled by the thesis, while the essay diverts from topic occasionally.

_____ The writer makes use of two to four sources.

_____ The sources are correctly documented and integrated into the wording of the essay with signal phrases.

_____ The paper has a clear organization that doesn't leave the reader wondering where the essay is headed.

_____ The paper has no consistent problems with grammar, mechanics, spelling, punctuation, or sentence structure.

D–Inadequate or Incompetent

D work falls short of three or more of the requirements for *C* work, and/or it may reflect the following:

_____ The writer failed to meet the requirements of the assignment.

_____ The paper contains consistent problems with grammar, mechanics, spelling, punctuation, or sentence structure that hinder the reader's progress through the essay.

_____ The organization of individual paragraphs is problematic.

_____ The organization of the overall essay is problematic.

F–Completely Unacceptable or Failing

The problems are with content, structure, and mechanics. This writing is characterized by any of the following: unclear purpose; incoherent organization; inadequate, irrelevant, or illogical development; little originality of thought; reliance on clichés; inappropriate word choice; ineffective or incorrect sentence structure; numerous or significant problems with mechanics and grammar. Plagiarism is also grounds for failure.

NUMBER GRADES

Use the following form to assess your own writing to determine your likely number grade.

PREWRITING [10 points]
☐ Writer shows evidence that he/she has considered ideas and their support.
☐ Writer submits an outline and at least **one rough draft** in addition to the final, clean copy.

ORGANIZATION AND DEVELOPMENT [50 POINTS]
☐ Writer creates a well-developed introduction that moves from general to specific information.
☐ Writer states the essay's thesis as the last sentence of the introduction.
☐ Writer composes a topic sentence for a body paragraph when introducing a new subtopic from the thesis statement.
☐ Writer **fully** develops each body paragraph by using facts, details, examples, and specific textual references taken from a close reading of the assigned literary selection.
☐ Writer uses transitions within and between paragraphs to organize logically the essay's information and to achieve coherence throughout the essay.
☐ Writer begins the conclusion with a reminder of the thesis statement.
☐ Writer composes the paper's last sentences to bring closure to the essay's central idea.
☐ Writer follows MLA format for the composition's final copy, which includes parenthetical documentation of outside resources when used and a "Works Cited" page listing those outside resources.

STYLE [20 points]

Central Idea

☐   Writer presents a significant and interesting central idea, clearly defined and supported with substantial, concrete, and consistently relevant details.

Sentence Structure

☐   Writer skillfully constructs sentences that display fluency, economy, and effective variety.

Diction

☐   Writer uses diction that is appropriate to the essay's subject, purpose, audience, and occasion; it is distinctive in precision, economy, and the idiomatic use of English.

MECHANICS AND USAGE [20 points]

☐ Capitalization	☐ Punctuation	☐ Spelling
☐ Pronoun Usage	☐ Pronoun/ Antecedent Agreement	☐ Verb Tense
☐ Subject/Verb Agreement		☐ Word Meaning
☐ Omission of Words	☐ Adjective/Adverb Usage	
	☐ Misplaced/Dangling Modifiers	

ANSWER KEY

Answers to many of the pages will vary. Here are answers to the questions that have definitive answers.

Page 4

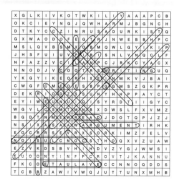

Page 37

1. additionally
2. although
3. besides
4. consequently
5. eventually
6. finally
7. however
8. initially
9. meanwhile
10. previously
11. similarly
12. since
13. therefore
14. unlike
15. while

Page 38

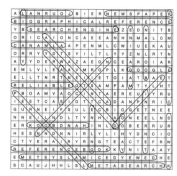

Page 39

1. 500s
2. 300s
3. Philosophy and Psychology
4. 800s
5. 200s
6. Geography and History
7. Fine Arts
8. 600s
9. Language
10. General Works

Page 42

1. c
2. b
3. a
4. e
5. f
6. d

Pages 44 and 45

1. "I think I'm gonna be sad."
2. Answers may vary.
3. Santorio
4. Hattie McDaniel
5. Mt. Whitney
6. Charles Martin Hall

Page 46

1. c
2. b
3. a

Page 49

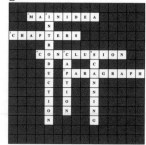

Page 51

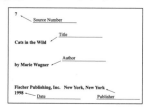

Page 52

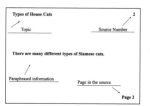

Page 66

1. XIX
2. 13
3. 15
4. 30
5. 9
6. 7
7. XXVI
8. 6
9. 31
10. 11
11. I
12. 20
13. 14
14. 4
15. XVII
16. 18
17. 8

18. 2
19. XII
20. 10
21. III
22. 24
23. 29
24. 25
25. XXVII
26. 16
27. 28
28. 5
29. 22
30. 21

Page 67

A
(b)
(2)
(a)
(1)
2
a
B
II
A

Page 85

1. Education in the Early Republic
2. New England Federalism
3. Trade with China in the Early Nineteenth Century
4. Causes of the Civil War
5. Historic Preservation in the Twentieth Century
6. American Pottery
7. American Impressionism
8. The Life of Mark Twain

Page 86

1. c
2. c
3. b

Page 87

1. not common knowledge
2. common knowledge
3. common knowledge
4. common knowledge
5. common knowledge

Page 89

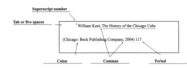

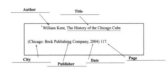

Page 94

Page 95

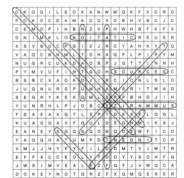

Pages 96 and 97

1. Please don't bother me because I've had a hard day.
2. *To Kill a Mockingbird* was set in the town of Maycomb, Alabama.
3. Paula and I are going to study Thursday night for the big test in History.
4. The War of 1812 ended on Saturday, December 24, 1814.
5. When you go to the store, please get some Purina Puppy Chow.
6. The pool will open for the summer on Saturday.
7. "We can have a city-wide picnic on Labor Day," Mayor White suggested.
8. Will you sign up to work at the Spring Fling?
9. We are visiting the Navajo Indian reservation.
10. We are reading a book about Mother Teresa.
11. There was a huge fire in Yellowstone National Park.
12. The Painted Desert has many beautiful colors.
13. Don't think I'll let you get away with that!
14. Wednesday was named for Woden, the Norse god of war.
15. Easter is always on Sunday.
16. My hamsters are named Sugarfoot and Raisin.
17. Our school supply list stated that we need Mead notebook paper.
18. I'd like you to meet Professor Timothy Adams.
19. We are taking a vacation to the West Coast.
20. He said, "We will be talking about the Great Depression."

Page 98

Page 99

1. Long ago, people thought the world's surface was flat.
2. The lamp's switch is broken.
3. Georgia's award is displayed in a frame.
4. Why did Matthew's attitude change?
5. Who said the actor's performance was bad?
6. Hawaii's volcanoes have been active recently.
7. We searched the quarry's rubble for arrowheads.
8. The school's playground now has picnic tables.
9. Six kittens were born to Mark's pet cat.
10. David's plan is to hire more painters to finish the job.

Page 100

1. Although he promised to build the treehouse, I'll probably have to.
2. Carla said that we're like family to her.
3. Since there'll be more sales after Labor Day, I'll go shopping then.
4. I wonder who's making all the noise.
5. You aren't going to stay out late tonight.
6. Sandra just couldn't stay away from the chocolate cakes.
7. That'll be the best way to solve our problems.
8. You told me you've never

been to the zoo.
9. "He isn't the fastest runner," she said.
10. "We didn't forget your birthday," the children said.

Page 101

1. My grandfather served in World War II, the Korean War, and the Vietnam War.
2. This week I am going to the dentist, having dinner with Grace, and taking the dog to the vet.
3. What are the capitals of Illinois, Alabama, and New Mexico?
4. Please choose a book, sit down, and read quietly until the bell rings.
5. We had pancakes, eggs, and bacon for breakfast this morning.
6. We haven't decided whether to fish, see a movie, or take a trip.
7. School, her job, and piano practice took up all of Gloria's time.
8. My mom sings jazz, gospel, and blues.
9. Would you like burgers, pizza, or pasta for dinner?
10. Darla is taking a trip to New York, New Jersey, and Connecticut.

Page 102

1. The house, they say, is haunted.
2. The field was a sunny, green meadow!
3. Garfield was a grumpy, annoying cat.
4. Bill looks peaceful when he is asleep, doesn't he?
5. The tiny, determined ant climbed the hill with the crumbs.
6. The stickers had fallen off the old, dusty paper.
7. Since she was the last person in line, she had to turn off the

lights.
8. Before I meet with your boss, please tell me a little bit about her.
9. To find all the treats, the children looked in every hiding place.
10. The woodpecker, however, lost its nest in the storm.

Page 103

1. Christopher Columbus and his men sailed from Lisbon, Portugal.
2. Mardi Gras is celebrated in New Orleans, Louisiana.
3. Danny has grandparents in Dublin, Ireland.
4. The Museum of Modern Art is in New York City, New York.
5. My daughter was born in Oslo, Norway.
6. I am going to visit my grandmother on April 4, 2007.
7. The hospital was dedicated on August 28, 1965.
8. The baby was born on September 27, 1996.
9. Massachusetts became a state on February 6, 1788.
10. Apollo 11 lifted off on July 16, 1969.

Page 104

1. dash
2. dash
3. hyphen
4. dash
5. hyphen
6. hyphen
7. dash
8. dash
9. hyphen
10. dash

Page 106

1. Everybody knows that broccoli provides your body with vitamin C.

2. The gymnasts shocked <u>their</u> audience with their amazing moves.
3. Either the lady or her mother gave <u>her</u> permission to pick flowers.
4. The computer and the video game have made <u>their</u> mark on modern life.
5. Which member of the boys' track team will beat <u>his</u> old record?
6. The volunteers for the dance received praise for <u>their</u> work.
7. The dry cleaner restored my filthy pants to <u>their</u> original condition.
8. The puppy and his mother cry until <u>their</u> owner feeds them.

Page 107
1. they
2. he
3. they
4. her
5. her
6. he
7. their
8. he
9. I
10. their

Pages 108 and 109
1. unclear
2. clear
3. unclear
4. clear
5. clear
6. unclear
7. unclear
8. unclear
9. unclear
10. clear
11. clear
12. unclear
13. clear
14. unclear
15. clear
16. unclear

Pages 110 and 111
1. him
2. us
3. they
4. We
5. her
6. her
7. them
8. I
9. he
10. he
11. them
12. she
13. her
14. They
15. We
16. us
17. her
18. I
19. we
20. us

Pages 112 and 113
1. spoke
2. failed
3. married
4. thought
5. ran
6. works
7. grows
8. have
9. call
10. shops
11. will knit
12. will finish
13. will have
14. will eat
15. will purchase

Page 114
1. had lived
2. had brushed
3. had cleaned
4. had learned
5. have washed
6. have worked
7. have finished
8. have asked
9. will have planted
10. will have waited
11. will have traveled
12. will have started

Page 115
agitated; agitated
notched; notching
delayed; delaying
embarrassed; embarrassing
cuddled; cuddling
braced; bracing
jeering; jeering
persisting; persisting
metered; metering
gazing; gazing
heaved; heaving
filtered; filtering
lectured; lecturing
oozing; oozing

Pages 116 and 117
1. b
2. a
3. a
4. c
5. b
6. c
7. c
8. c
9. b
10. a
11. b
12. a
13. a
14. b
15. c
16. c
17. b
18. c
19. a
20. a

Pages 118 and 119
1. seem
2. wants
3. boards
4. believes
5. belong
6. is

7. auditions
8. hopes
9. has
10. know
11. understand
12. is
13. play
14. are
15. wants
16. love
17. cooks
18. fix
19. cheers
20. wonders

Page 120 and 121

1. As baked beans and potato salad slid onto Manny's new shoes.
2. Ever since Andrea peeked at Melinda's paper during the algebra quiz.
3. Which caused a package of berries to fall to the floor.
4. For example, Kerry's poodle, Maizy, or Greta's collie, Kia.
5. But was too shy to raise her hand and give an answer.
6. Although she didn't want to leave in the middle of the lecture.
7. To memorize the vocabulary for his science test.
8. Chewing the dry, crumbly, rye toast bought at the health food store.
9. Where his nose sniffs all around looking for crumbs that we might have dropped.
10. Bucking and rearing like a wild horse that cowboys had captured.

Page 122 and 123

1. We bought shoes, clothes, towels, and swimsuits at the store. Fortunately, we have a large suitcase for the trip.
2. The young child seemed to be lost. She was crying and looking for her grandma.
3. My mother retired from the Army last year. She is writing a book about her career.
4. Inspector Green came to our school. He showed us some of his equipment and talked about the Treasury Department.
5. My nephew grew three inches in one year. Now he is much better at basketball.
6. I have to clean my room. I have to make my bed before I catch the bus for school.
7. Marta wanted help with the recipe. She couldn't make the dish alone.
8. We went to my cousin's wedding in Virginia. Over 300 people were at the reception.
9. Our baseball team won the tournament last week. We had to go into extra innings to win.
10. Janelle's birthday is on October 6. She is going to the Fall Festival for her birthday celebration.
11. Kyla and Johnny worked very hard on their book report. They felt they earned a better grade.
12. We will be on our annual trip to the shore next week. We will not be able to attend the parade.

Pages 124 and 125

1. they're
2. lose
3. weather
4. compliment
5. There
6. principles
7. Lay
8. too
9. loose
10. affect
11. whose
12. to; two
13. It's
14. their
15. too
16. they're
17. You're
18. than
19. then
20. dual

Pages 126 and 127

1. vacuum
2. vacancy
3. wholly
4. sovereign
5. shriek
6. specify
7. vacillate
8. suppress
9. sufficient
10. unskillful
11. threshold
12. superintendent
13. beautiful
14. commitment
15. all right
16. quizzed
17. noticeable
18. newsstand
19. sincerely
20. different

Pages 128 and 129

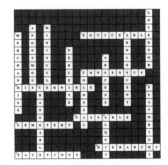